TWENTIETH CENTURY PEOPLE

FRANKLIN D. ROOSEVELT

NOTHING TO FEAR BUT FEAR

D1556064

TWENTIETH CENTURY PEOPLE

ROALD AMUNDSEN: First to the South Pole
Margaret J. Miller
WINSTON CHURCHILL: Never Surrender
William Vivian Butler
MARIE CURIE: A Life for Science
Ruth Brandon
HENRY FORD: The Motor Man
Barbara Stoney
AMY JOHNSON: Queen of the Air
Gordon Snell
MONTGOMERY OF ALAMEIN: The General Who Never Lost a Campaign
John O. H. Fisher
ANNA PAVLOVA: A Legend Among Dancers
Robina Beckles Willson
FRANKLIN D. ROOSEVELT: Nothing to Fear but Fear
William Vivian Butler

TWENTIETH CENTURY PEOPLE

FRANKLIN D. ROOSEVELT

NOTHING TO FEAR BUT FEAR

BY WILLIAM VIVIAN BUTLER

HODDER AND STOUGHTON
LONDON   SYDNEY   AUCKLAND   TORONTO

British Library Cataloguing in Publication Data

Butler, William Vivian
   Franklin D. Roosevelt. – (Twentieth century
   people)
   1. Roosevelt, Franklin Delano
   2. Presidents – United States – Biography
   – Juvenile literature
   I. Title   II. Series
   973.917′092′4   E807

   ISBN 0-340-27097-7

Published by Hodder & Stoughton Children's Books, (a division of
Hodder & Stoughton Ltd), Mill Road, Dunton Green, Sevenoaks,
Kent TN13 2YJ. Printed by Morrison & Gibb Ltd, London and Edinburgh.
Photoset by Rowland Phototypesetting Ltd, Bury St Edmunds, Suffolk.

Contents

For CAROL
and KEN

1

 Golden Spoon

If ever a baby was born with a silver spoon in his mouth, it was Franklin Delano Roosevelt. It would not be too much to describe his as a golden one.

The birth took place on January 30, 1882, in the stylish Roosevelt family home, Springwood, Hyde Park, about eighty miles from New York.

The doctor accidentally gave Roosevelt's mother an overdose of chloroform (a little-understood drug in those days) and she and the baby nearly died. But apart from this difficulty in actually getting born, Roosevelt had a serene and trouble-free childhood, cushioned by the enormous wealth of his family from all the ordinary shocks of early life.

His father, James, was an immensely successful businessman, who virtually owned a big American railway. It is said that he was a typical nineteenth-century American gentleman, who 'smoked his cheroot with a fine air', but not much else is remembered about him. We do know that he was old enough to be Roosevelt's grandfather, and yet was a very active sportsman, teaching his son to ride, hunt, swim, sail boats and (in winter) to skate and sleigh. He took the family on frequent journeys around the United States, travelling in their own private railway coach, complete with several luxurious bedrooms, a sitting room, a kitchen, and a steward whose speciality was making 'egg bread', an American delicacy which Roosevelt loved.

Apart from travelling all over the U.S. in the family coach, Roosevelt was taken to Europe every year by his parents; and these were not just visits, but often included bizarre adventures. (One day, while bicycling through the Black Forest with his private tutor, Roosevelt was arrested four times by the German police in a single afternoon – once for knocking over a noticeboard, once for picking cherries, once for parking his bicycle outside a railway station, and once for cycling after sunset.)

James Roosevelt gave his son a pony when he was four, a horse when he was ten, a gun of his own when he was twelve and a yacht as soon as he was old enough to sail it. The boy went everywhere with his father, even down to the village every morning to collect the mail.

His mother, Sara, was herself the daughter of a millionaire, Wallace Delano II. She was richer in her own right than her husband, and was as determined as James to see that Franklin should have everything he needed.

With a rich, railway-tycoon father and a doting, millionairess mother, it is hardly surprising that Roosevelt was not brought up like other children. He lived at home on the thousand-acre Roosevelt estate, surrounded by servants and taught by private tutors until he was fourteen. For all that time, he hardly saw any other child who wasn't a Roosevelt, or from some equally rich family. Roosevelt was particularly fond of his cousin Eleanor, a very serious, rather ugly little girl whom he used to carry pick-a-back around the house when he was four and she was two.

Top left: *Roosevelt as a baby, held aloft by his proud father, James Roosevelt.*
(Oliver Yates Collection). Top right: *With his mother Sara Delano Roosevelt, a
millionairess in her own right* and below: *Springwood, Hyde Park, centre of the
thousand-acre Roosevelt estate. Here Roosevelt lived, surrounded by servants
and taught by private tutors, until he was fourteen.* (Peter Newark's Western
Americana)

There were plenty of other Roosevelt children to see. There were eight or nine other branches of the Roosevelt family, all of them rich, and all living within an hour or so's coach-ride from Springwood. The Roosevelts had come from Holland in the early Colonial days, two centuries before, and had amassed so much money, and bought so many thousands of acres of land, that they had become a kind of aristocracy. They were regarded as the height of high society, setting the rest of the nation an example in how to live graciously and behave with style. It was normal for the Roosevelts to hobnob with Presidents, and Roosevelt was taken by his father to the White House to meet President Grover Cleveland when he was only four or five.

It seems that the Roosevelts called on an awkward day. Cleveland was up to his eyes in work, and feeling very sorry for himself. He had hardly any time to talk to his visitors at all. He simply patted the young Roosevelt on the head, and made a remark that has gone down in history.

'There's just one thing I wish for you, little boy. And that is that you never become President of the United States!'

If Cleveland had had his wish, the United States would have lost perhaps the greatest President that she has ever known.

* * *

Sometimes Sunday afternoon would be an alarming time for Roosevelt. One of his distant relatives would come to tea: a fifth cousin named Theodore. Cousin Teddy, as he was called, was a ferocious, thick-set, red-faced man – old enough to be Roosevelt's uncle – who never spoke without roaring, and who strode about the house as though he was making a series of cavalry charges from room to room.

Cousin Teddy's favourite trick was to pick Roosevelt up bodily, put him under his arm, and charge out on to the landing, roaring 'It's time this little piggy went to market!' Roosevelt was terrified that at any moment he might be dropped over the banisters or down the stairs.

Theodore, it was explained to him, came from a rather wild side of the family, known as the Knickerbocker Roosevelts. They weren't smooth and civilised, like the Hyde Park Roosevelts, to whom *he* belonged.

Smooth and civilised was, from all accounts, the sort of boy that Franklin Roosevelt was growing up to be.

He was very friendly and good-natured; seldom lost his temper; rarely got into any sort of trouble or mischief – and was remembered by almost everyone who knew him at the time as being really rather colourless and dull.

On occasions, though, he could surprise everybody – even his own mother – by suddenly and quite unexpectedly taking command.

Once Sara watched him playing with a crowd of children (mostly Roosevelts, as usual) and noticed that he seemed to be laying down the law the whole time. She asked him why in the world he had suddenly turned so bossy. He shrugged, smiled his smooth Roosevelt smile, and explained rather plaintively: 'It's just that if I don't give the orders, nothing ever happens!'

11

One other thing about the young Roosevelt was rather unusual. From his earliest years, he had a deep fascination with the sea. It was almost as if something was telling him that water was going to play a big part in his life. He read all the books on naval history that he could get his hands on, and by the time he was fourteen was expert on every sea war that the United States had ever fought. He pleaded with his father to be allowed to join the Navy, but James told him sternly that he was born to be a landowner, and must stay at home to look after the family estates. The best thing he could do was study law, the proper profession for an American gentleman.

Typically, Roosevelt did not argue or make a scene. From all accounts, he just grinned amiably and said: 'If that's the way you want it, Pops . . .' ('Pops' was what he always called his father.)

Now that he was fourteen, it was time at last to leave the feathered Roosevelt nest and go to boarding-school. The family had put his name down for Groton, one of the most exclusive private schools in the United States, attended by only about 150 boys, all of them from wealthy families.

Life at Groton was altogether tougher than anything he had been used to. The boys lived in bare, cell-like cubicles. They had to rise at 7 a.m., and take a cold shower first thing every day. Great emphasis was laid on good manners. At bedtime, all the boys had to queue up in their best suits, with stiff collars and highly-polished shoes, just to shake hands with the headmaster and his wife, and wish them good-night.

This headmaster, the Reverend Endicott Peabody,

seems to have been quite a character. In a squeaky, high-pitched voice, he lectured the boys endlessly on how, being rich and privileged children, they all ought to go into politics and fight for the rights of the *under*privileged – the poor, the starving, the unemployed.

Most of the boys at Groton laughed at the good Reverend. Some of them even hated him, and called him a 'traitor to his class'. But Roosevelt listened to him with great attention. He had absolutely no idea what it meant to be poor or starving or unemployed, but he certainly agreed that the underprivileged should be helped, and that it was the duty of the rich to help them.

Roosevelt was very much an outsider at Groton. Every single boy apart from him was a Republican – a supporter of the businessman's political party. But Roosevelt, like his father and mother, was a Democrat – a supporter of the party which believed in reforming the country to give a better chance to the poor. Boys who dare to be different usually have to pay for it, and Roosevelt was no exception. He was made to dance in a corner of the classroom, while the older boys hacked at his shins with hockey-sticks. His enemies soon gave up this bullying, though. Roosevelt's sunny nature took all the point out of it. Instead of getting angry, he hopped about nimbly, and appeared to be enjoying the whole thing.

In other words, Roosevelt at school was not very different from the boy he had been at home: friendly, extraordinarily good-tempered – but colourless. The other boys ended by respecting him, and even liking him – but none of them became close friends of his. He wasn't good enough at sports. He didn't seem to see things their way. And they didn't really like his smooth, Hyde-Park-Roosevelt manner; his refusal to get upset by anything or anybody. In the America of those days – as Hollywood Westerns still remind us – to be really admired, you had to be rough, tough and preferably rather wild.

At just about this time, a national leader appeared who was so unbelievably rough, tough and wild that he became overnight the hero of all America. He was none other than Roosevelt's Cousin Teddy, the man who had so often nearly dropped him over the banisters when he was small.

Theodore Roosevelt had entered politics with all

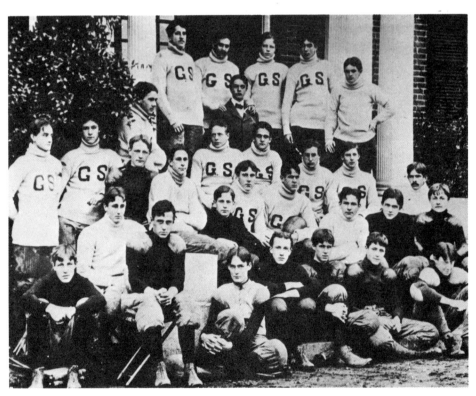

Roosevelt (second from left, front row) as an unhappy footballer at Groton School. (Oliver Yates Collection)

Colonel Theodore Roosevelt, the distant cousin who became the hero of all America. (BBC Hulton)

the force of a stampeding elephant – a Republican elephant, incidentally: only the Hyde Park Roosevelts were Democrats. In 1896 (the year Franklin went to Groton) Theodore had become Assistant Secretary to the U.S. Navy, although he did not concern himself much with naval affairs. At that time a revolution was going on in the Spanish colony of Cuba, and Theodore went stumping up and down the nation, thundering that the United States ought to go to the aid of the gallant Cubans, in their fight for freedom against the Spanish tyrants. The thought of war seemed to excite Theodore. 'Great masterful races have always been *fightin'* races,' he roared at his audiences, crashing his fist into his palm, and looking ready to strike down anyone who disagreed with him. 'No triumph of peace is quite so great as the supreme triumph of war!'

15

Theodore got his way, and two years later – in 1898 – the United States did in fact declare war on the Spaniards in Cuba. It was proposed to send a regular army there, which would have been quite enough to deal with the situation. But Theodore insisted on raising a volunteer cavalry regiment, which became known as the 'Rough Riders'. All kinds of people rushed to volunteer. Polo players from high society mingled with hordes of cowboys from the genuine old Wild West, whooping and hollering and firing their six-shooters as though they were taking part in a rodeo.

'This sure is a jim-dandy regiment,' roared Theodore. 'And we're gonna fight a mighty bully war.'

And that is precisely what he did. The Spanish-American War was over in six months, and its most famous moment came when Theodore – now a full Colonel – led the Rough Riders in a spectacular charge up San Juan Hill.

The part the regular army played in beating the Spaniards was forgotten. As far as the U.S. public was concerned, the war had been won by Colonel Teddy Roosevelt virtually single-handed. Photographs of Theodore appeared on mantelpieces throughout the country. Legends about him spread like wildfire. It was said that he was so tough he often fought grizzly bears with his fists. When, some time later, it was realised that he was very tender-hearted towards bear cubs, and regarded them as pets, millions of U.S. children were given toy bears in his honour – and toy bears have been called Teddy bears ever since.

In 1900, Theodore became Vice-President, the

The capture of San Juan Hill by Colonel Roosevelt's Rough Riders during the Spanish-American War. Most Americans thought Theodore won the war almost single-handed. (Peter Newark's Western Americana)

second most important man in the country after the President himself, William McKinley.

That was the year when Theodore's young, apparently colourless cousin left Groton to go to the famous American university, Harvard. It is not known what Franklin Roosevelt thought about Cousin Teddy becoming the most popular man in the United States. But it is known that he supported the Cuban War. When it was at its height, he planned to run away from Groton and join the Army. Perhaps he even intended volunteering as a Rough Rider. But, typically, he caught measles at just the wrong moment, and found himself spending weeks in the school sanatorium instead.

Big things, though, were about to happen in Franklin Roosevelt's smooth and tranquil world. The four years he spent at Harvard (1900–1904) were among the most important of his life.

17

In December, 1900, his father James – his constant companion during his childhood – suddenly died. His mother, heartbroken, decided that from now onwards, she would devote her whole life to helping her boy get on. She actually took a house close to Harvard so that she could keep him constantly under her eye. Some boys might have felt that they were being mother-smothered. But Roosevelt, gently obliging as ever, raised no objection. His mother's place came in handy, anyway; he frequently took room-mates back there for dinner at nights.

Then, in the September of 1901, an event occurred that shook the United States to its foundations. President McKinley was making a speech in Buffalo when he was shot three times by a mad assassin. For days, leading doctors struggled to save his life; but they quarrelled with each other, and blundered badly over the treatment. Exactly a week after the shooting, McKinley died, and at that moment, under U.S. law, Cousin Theodore automatically became President of the United States.

Two years later, in 1903, something happened which had an even greater effect on Roosevelt's future. For a long time, he had been secretly going round with Eleanor, the 'ugly-duckling' cousin to whom he had given pick-a-back rides at the age of four. Now he suddenly announced to his mother that he and Eleanor were in love, and wanted to get married as soon as possible.

Sara Roosevelt was horrified at the idea of her beloved boy getting married at the tender age of twenty-two. That winter, she commanded him to take a break from Harvard, and accompany her on a long cruise to the West Indies, in the hope that travel would put romance right out of his mind. Roosevelt amiably agreed to go – but on his return he announced, equally amiably, that he was more determined to marry Eleanor than ever. Sara simply had to put up with the situation, but a subtle battle of wills began between her and Eleanor which one day was to turn into a full-scale tug of war.

Like Theodore Roosevelt, Eleanor came from the wild Knickerbocker side of the family. All through childhood, life had been as rough on her as it had been easy on Franklin. Her mother had died suddenly of diphtheria when she was only eight. Her father, around whom all her hopes of happiness were now centred, began to drink too much, and had to go to a home for treatment. Eleanor was sent to live with her grandmother, and although she begged and pleaded to see her father, she was never allowed near him again. Shortly after this, in any event, he died – not from drink, but from a brain tumour. All this turned Eleanor into a daydreamer, and for year after year during her teens, she had pretended that her father was beside her – an invisible companion wherever she went.

Perhaps because of their different backgrounds, Franklin and Eleanor had completely opposite characters. Roosevelt was sunny, easygoing, tolerant, always convinced that somehow, everything would turn out fine. Eleanor was intensely serious and determined. Perhaps this very seriousness was what attracted him to her; perhaps he wanted to learn the secret of that determination. And Eleanor, after all her troubles, must have been sorely in need of that ever-reassuring Roosevelt smile.

19

Eleanor was very fond of doing good works – of a rather individual kind. Once a week she would visit a social centre in New York – to teach gymnastics and ballet-dancing to the poor!

On one occasion, she took Roosevelt with her. It was probably the first time this millionaire's son had ever travelled by bus. It was certainly the first time he had ever seen slums. He stood, thunderstruck, staring at the rows of grimy houses, so overcrowded that families of fifteen or sixteen were often packed into a single room.

'My God!' he muttered. 'I had no *idea* people lived like this!'

That may well have been the moment when the crusading Roosevelt was born: the Roosevelt who was to do more for the poor people of the United States than any other President, before or since.

At the time, though, it just looked as if he was going to be sick on the pavement . . . sick with a mixture of disgust and anger. He knew now that Dr Peabody had been right. Something had to be done – and it was up to privileged people like him to do it.

At long, long last, the very rich young man had met the very poor, and felt he had a cause to fight for.

But he had never had to fight hard for anything in his life, and simply did not know how or where to begin.

For a long time, it looked as though he might never begin at all.

2

 ## Background
Roar

Eleanor did not only take Roosevelt to the slums. Quite often he went with her to the White House, the official home of U.S. Presidents. She could come and go there as often as she pleased, because she was President Theodore Roosevelt's favourite niece. (He and his family had often had her over to stay when she was a little girl. Teddy used to try and teach her to swim by the simple process of hurling her into a river and seeing what happened. But he always had to jump in and rescue her, puffing and bellowing – because she never failed to sink like a stone.)

As Franklin's cousin and Eleanor's uncle, Theodore provided the young couple's lives with a constant background roar. He agreed to come to the wedding and give the bride away. The trouble was, the moment Teddy arrived on the scene, the bride and groom got hardly any attention at all. Huge crowds lined the street outside to cheer: 'Hooray for Teddy. Ain't he the real thing!' Immediately after the ceremony (which was conducted, by the way, by the Rev. Endicott Peabody) Teddy felt like a drink. He charged off into the refreshment room and all the guests followed, leaving a forlorn and forgotten Franklin and Eleanor to bring up the rear.

Roosevelt didn't appear to mind. As usual, he was amiable to all – but legend says that he was

inwardly furious, and that that was the moment when he secretly decided that one day he would be a 'fine and dandy bully President' himself.

The Roosevelts honeymooned in England, to find that even there, they couldn't escape from Theodore. Brown's Hotel in London mistakenly thought that Franklin *was* the President, and had got the Royal Suite ready, festooned with U.S. flags.

Franklin and Eleanor returned to the States a few months later – to a house bought and furnished throughout by Sara Roosevelt, who had installed herself in the premises next door! Eleanor tried hard to make her husband understand that it wasn't nice for a bride to run a home, however beautiful, in which everything had been chosen by her mother-in-law. But he just grinned, told her she was making a silly fuss about nothing, and left the room. Eleanor, used all her life to the tough Knickerbocker Roosevelts, must have wondered if she had married a man with any fight in him at all.

By this time, Roosevelt had left Harvard (where he had done reasonably, but not spectacularly, well) and had become a partner in a firm of lawyers. He was still following the advice his father had given him when he was fourteen. It seemed as if all he was aiming to do was settle down as a typical landown-ing gentleman, handling a few legal cases on the side.

Meanwhile, Teddy was continuing to dazzle the country with firework displays of personality and drive. In 1904, he fought a roistering election campaign – everywhere he went he had bands play 'There's a Hot Time In The Old Town Tonight' – and was returned as President with a big majority.

Eleanor on her wedding day. It was Cousin Teddy who really stole the show!
(BBC Hulton)

During his next term of office, he made the United States a power to be reckoned with, sending the navy around the world for the first time; creating the Republic of Panama, and building the Panama Canal. At the end, in 1908, he could have been President for a third time with no trouble at all. But no President had stood for a third term before, and Theodore felt it would be greedy to want to do so. 'I think the American people feel a little tired of me, a feeling with which I entirely sympathise,' he roared, and stood down, persuading an old friend and colleague, Senator William Howard Taft, to run for President instead. Once Taft was elected, Teddy charged off on a year-long African safari, during which he shot 296 unfortunate animals, amongst them five elephants, thirteen rhino and seven hippopotami.

While his cousin was giving the African wild life a hot time in the old jungle, Franklin Roosevelt was beginning to find life as a lawyer just a little tame, even for him. One day a Democrat politician called Ed Perkins drove up to his house in a shiny red Maxwell roadster – one of the most flashy of the very early cars. He had come to ask Roosevelt if he would stand as a Senator – a member of the senior half of the U.S. parliament.

Roosevelt found himself strongly tempted.

'But,' he said mildly, 'I'll – er – have to talk it over with my mother first.'

Ed Perkins stared. Could this possibly be a relative of the great Theodore?

He thrust out his jaw.

'Now, look,' he said. 'I've got a lot of important men waiting for your answer. Do you really want me to go back and tell them that you had to ask your mother?'

Roosevelt gulped and swallowed hard. Then he made a quick decision. (He had, all his life, a surprising talent for making those.)

'All right,' he said. 'I'll stand.'

A lot of people in the Democrat party thought that Ed had made a big mistake in choosing Roosevelt. They thought he was a lightweight, a sissy. But they soon discovered that there was nothing sissified about Franklin Roosevelt when it came to fighting elections. To start with, he insisted on taking over Ed's Maxwell roadster, and caused a sensation by campaigning in it everywhere. He was almost the first politician to campaign from a car. He discovered

Left: *Theodore Roosevelt as President. He filled Franklin's and Eleanor's lives with a constant background roar.* Right: *Roosevelt as a Junior Senator. People thought he was too mild a young man to get very far in politics.* (Peter Newark's Western Americana)

that most of the voters were farmers, and went to immense pains to find out answers to local farm problems. And this aristocrat of aristocrats charmed everyone he met by smiling, shaking hands and saying 'Call me Franklin'. He started every speech with the words 'My friends . . .' and somehow gave the voters the feeling that that was just how he thought of them. Although no Democrat had ever won in that area before, he was returned with a 1,140 majority.

So Roosevelt became a Junior Senator. But there didn't seem to be much chance of his getting any further in politics, because, for many years now, the other party – the Republicans – had been in power, led for most of the time by that arch-Republican, Theodore Roosevelt.

But in a couple of years, all that was to change – and it was Theodore Roosevelt himself who changed it. Coming back from his African safari, Teddy didn't like what he'd heard about the way Taft was running the country, and he suddenly decided to stand against him at the next Presidental election. (In the U.S. Presidents are elected every four years.) To do this, Teddy started a brand-new political party of his own, called, believe it or not, the Bull Moose Party.

The next election came in 1912. It was a strange, three-cornered contest. Taft stood as a Republican. Woodrow Wilson stood as a Democrat. And Teddy Roosevelt went roaring up and down the country as a 'Bull Moose'. It was in the course of this campaign, incidentally, that Teddy put on the most courageous performance of his life.

He was on his way to a lecture hall when a fanatic called Joseph Shrank suddenly whipped out a Colt revolver, and shot him in the chest at six-foot range. Fortunately, Teddy happened to have all the notes for his speech in his breast pocket. It was a long speech – the notes went on for fifty pages – and they, together with a spectacle-case, took the main force of the bullet. Teddy was knocked flat on his back, but managed to get up again. There was a terrible pain in his chest, and his shirt felt wet with blood; but when he coughed, no blood came out of his mouth, and so he was fairly certain the bullet hadn't entered a lung.

He roared at the crowd to stand back from the culprit, went over to him, and said quite kindly: 'You poor scoundrel!' Then he caused a sensation by flatly refusing to get into an ambulance. 'I do not care a rap about being shot, not a rap,' he barked, walking on towards the lecture hall. 'I have a message to deliver and will deliver it as long as there is breath in my body . . .'

And deliver it he did – for all of fifty minutes – with friends standing round to catch him if he fainted. Astonishingly, he did not faint – although it was discovered afterwards that there was a bullet wedged in a muscle four inches deep in his chest.

Even in his hospital bed, nothing could stop Teddy roaring. 'Tell the people not to worry about me. If I go down, another will take my place. For always, the army is true! Always, the cause is there!'

It was almost as if he knew that the Theodore Roosevelt era was over. Although he recovered completely from the shooting, he did not win the election, and never played a big part in U.S. politics again. But he had seen to it that the now-hated Taft was out of the White House. He had also succeeded in

Roosevelt was never happier than when he was close to water – swimming, sailing or (as here) canoeing at Campobello. (Oliver Yates Collection)

splitting the Republican vote down the middle. As a result, America had a Democrat as President again: Woodrow Wilson.

One of Wilson's first acts was to offer an important government post to an amiable young Senator who had worked hard on his behalf all through the campaign.

Franklin D. Roosevelt suddenly found himself Assistant Secretary to the U.S. Navy. In other words, he was in the very position which had provided Teddy with his first step towards the White House – although hardly anyone imagined that the new Roosevelt was going to make it all the way.

Where was the guts? Where was the gusto? Where was the Teddy Roosevelt *fire*?

3

 # The Risk-taker

As a matter of fact, there was no lack of gusto in Roosevelt's approach to his new job.

All his life, he had been crazy about the sea – and it must have struck him as funny that, after obeying his father and giving up all thought of joining the Navy, here he was second-in-command of all the nation's naval affairs! And before he finished, he was really first in command. The Secretary of the Navy, Joseph Daniels, was a hillbilly farming type who knew very little about ships and nothing at all about how to deal with admirals. He was often bewildered by his job and left more and more of the work in Roosevelt's hands.

Roosevelt, then, virtually ran the U.S. Navy for the period 1912–1920 – some of the darkest years in world history. He ran it in a typical Franklin D. Roosevelt way. He never threw his weight about; never banged the table or stormed out of a meeting, and very rarely had even a mild disagreement with anybody. He became personal friends of many of the admirals in the fleet, and – still more important – was liked by the workers in the U.S. shipyards, where there had been endless strikes and disputes in the past. But there was not one serious strike or controversy during the whole time that Roosevelt was in charge.

Somehow, in the friendly atmosphere he created in the Navy Department, decisions were taken at enormous speed – and few people noticed that those decisions were often daring and even reckless. Roosevelt would order a destroyer as casually as most men would buy a new tie. And he wouldn't lose a second's sleep over whether people higher up approved of what he was doing.

In August, 1914, the First World War began in Europe. Under its aggressive leader, Kaiser Wilhelm, Germany invaded Belgium and declared war on France. Britain rushed to the help of the Belgians and French, and for the next four years, the British and French armies were locked in an exhausting, bloody, seemingly endless struggle, bogged down in trenches and firing at the Germans across a few yards of barbed wire. Thousands of lives were lost every day, and even an advance of a few miles was considered a major victory.

At the same time, the Germans tried to starve Britain into surrender by using submarines (U-boats as they were called) to sink any ships bringing supplies to its shores.

Congress – the U.S. parliament – was determined to keep America out of the war, and so was Woodrow Wilson, a man who believed passionately that war was the worst thing that could happen to any nation.

Roosevelt, on the other hand, sided with Britain and France and their allies from the start. He felt hurt, he told his mother, that Kaiser Wilhelm should have left the United States out when he had declared war on everybody else. And, he added, 'I just *know* I shall do some awful unneutral thing before I get through!'

30

Roosevelt, Assistant Secretary of the Navy, with his boss Joseph Daniels, who disliked dealing with admirals and left it to Roosevelt to get the fleet ready for war. (Peter Newark's Western Americana)

He was determined that, if war came, the U.S.A. should have a Navy that was strong, armed to the teeth and, in particular, well-equipped to fight U-boats. All this meant ordering vast numbers of ships and supplies. Officially, every one of those orders had to be passed by Congress, which, as Roosevelt knew, would have turned most of them down. Over and over again, he stuck his neck out by giving orders by word-of-mouth and 'forgetting' to report them to Congress. Hundreds of millions of dollars were involved in those deals – and Roosevelt said later that if everything he'd done at the Navy Department became known, he'd be jailed for nine hundred and ninety-nine years.

In April, 1917, the whole situation changed. German U-boats were torpedoing so many unarmed American ships that, for this and other reasons, the

31

Franklin D. Roosevelt

United States found itself forced to declare war. (It is said that, after signing the declaration, Woodrow Wilson broke down and sobbed like a child, because he realised he would be bringing death to so many young men.) Suddenly, the one thing that mattered was that the U.S. Navy should be strong. Congress was not sorry to discover that, behind their backs and at great personal risk, Franklin D. Roosevelt had been quietly seeing to it that the United States had one of the most powerful fleets on earth.

*　　*　　*

Woodrow Wilson himself began to take an interest in his bright young Assistant Secretary to the Navy.

Woodrow Wilson, the President who 'sobbed like a child' when he had to declare war. (Peter Newark's Western Americana)

US submarine chasers – an idea of Franklin D. Roosevelt's which helped to win the U-boat war. (BBC Hulton)

He spent evening after evening having long meetings with him, during which they dreamt up an elaborate scheme for laying a vast minefield to bottle up the German navy. This scheme was never put into action – but Roosevelt did create a new, fast submarine-chasing boat, which played a big part in winning the U-boat war.

Now that the U.S. was in the fight, Roosevelt felt his old schoolboy urge to enlist in the Navy returning in force. But Woodrow Wilson vetoed the idea, every bit as sternly as James Roosevelt had done years before. 'Young man, your best service is definitely to stay right where you are,' he said. Roosevelt, as usual, didn't argue. He probably said 'Okay, Mr President,' as amiably as he had once drawled 'Okay, Pops'.

At about this time, another Roosevelt was pleading with the President for permission to take a personal hand in the war. Teddy – now once again Colonel Theodore – Roosevelt wanted to collect the old Rough Riders together and take them to Europe, to show the Huns some jim-dandy U.S. fighting. Woodrow Wilson flatly refused to give his consent, and no doubt he was right. You couldn't, after all, shout 'Charge!' and ride hell-for-leather across a No-Man's-Land of mud and barbed wire. The Teddy Roosevelt world had gone for ever, and it simply wasn't his kind of war they were fighting any more.

Although Colonel Theodore wasn't amongst them, U.S. troops poured into Europe in 1917 and 1918, exactly the kind of reinforcements that the desperate British and French had hoped and prayed for. With their help, World War I was ended, in November, 1918.

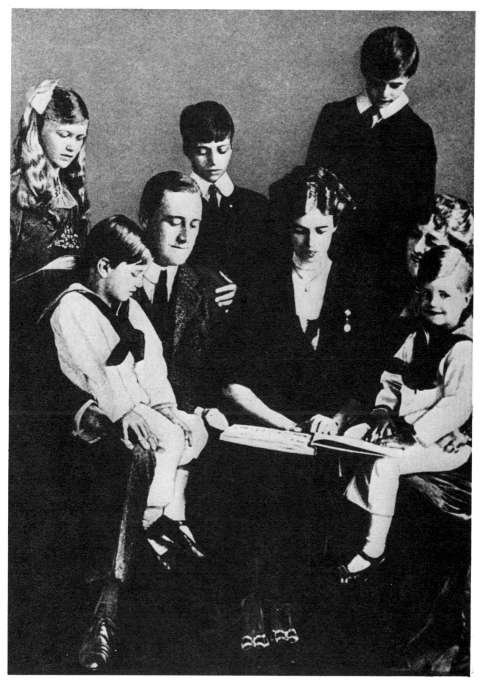

From a growing fleet to a growing family. A rare glimpse of Roosevelt's home life during his busy Navy days. (Peter Newark's Western Americana)

Franklin D. Roosevelt

A few months earlier, Franklin Roosevelt had finally succeeded in taking to the sea in a big way. In a destroyer – flying, amongst its other ensigns, his own personally-designed Roosevelt flag – he crossed the Atlantic to review the American fleet in Europe.

In the course of this visit, he was introduced one evening to Winston Churchill, who had been Britain's First Lord of the Admiralty (equivalent to the U.S. Secretary of the Navy) earlier in the War. Twenty years later, these two men were to form one of the most important friendships in the history of the world. But at this first meeting, they had nothing much to say to each other, and afterwards, Churchill never even remembered that they'd met.

Perhaps he'd expected a roaring Roosevelt, and believed this charming smiler to be just a colourless nobody.

It was a mistake that was soon to be made by the whole U.S.

4
The Icy Dip

The three years after the War began sadly for Roosevelt, and ended in tragedy and disaster.

In 1919, Cousin Teddy, broken-hearted after the death of his favourite son Quentin at the front, suddenly fell ill and a few nights later, died in his sleep. ('If he'd been awake at the time,' somebody said, 'there'd have been a hell of a fight.')

A year later, in 1920, Roosevelt was once again invited to follow Theodore's example and stand as Vice-President, supporting a Presidential candidate called James A. Cox.

Roosevelt fought a very energetic campaign, making over a thousand speeches around the country. The keynote, as always, was casual friendliness. After each speech, he would grin and tell the crowd: 'Come up and see me some time!' On quite a few occasions, he found himself being mistaken for Theodore's son. ('We voted for your old man, young feller, and by golly, we'll vote for you!' old Bull Moosers would shout.) Teddy's eldest son, Colonel Theodore Roosevelt Junior, was so enraged by this that he went on a speech-making tour, to point out that Franklin belonged to a different, and far inferior, branch of the family. Roosevelt thought this very funny, but Eleanor was so annoyed that she did not speak to any of the 'superior' Roosevelts for years.

Roosevelt in high spirits, shortly before disaster struck. Though, in spite of everything, it was not long before those high spirits returned. (Peter Newark's Western Americana)

Not that any of this mattered. Cox and Roosevelt totally failed to impress the American people. They lost the election so badly, in fact, that Roosevelt decided to leave politics altogether for the time being, and return to practising law.

There is no doubt that he was bitterly disappointed, although he tried to hide it and grin his way through, as usual. At last, at any rate, he could spend more time with Eleanor and the children. They had five by this time: one girl and four boys.

On August 10, 1921, Roosevelt took Eleanor and the four boys for a sail on a small yacht. He was teaching the boys how to handle it. Roosevelt was never the stern, dignified parent: halfway through, his teaching sessions always ended up with everyone horsing around. On this occasion, the horsing got too violent, and Roosevelt was knocked overboard, into the freezing waters of the Bay of Fundy.

Once again the sea was to play a big part in Roosevelt's life; but this time its role was a cruel one.

Roosevelt spent several minutes in the water

The losing double – in 1920, Roosevelt stood as Vice-President, supporting Presidential candidate James A. Cox (right). (BBC Hulton)

before he was rescued. He was blue all over and shivering violently; but soon he had recovered and was laughing the whole thing off.

The next day he took three of the children – the girl, Anna, and two of her brothers – out in another sailing boat, and again they had an adventure. They spotted a forest fire raging, and fought it with sticks for hours.

Having been freezing on the day before, Roosevelt was now hot and sticky, and felt burnt to a cinder. He decided to take a swim. Afterwards, coming out of the water, he walked back to the house, and found that the post – or as he would have called it, his mail – had arrived. Exhausted by now, he flopped down in a chair and spent half an hour reading his letters – still in his wet bathing suit.

Suddenly he tried to stand up, and found he couldn't. Sharp pains were shooting through his legs. He felt feverish, as though he was in for the flu.

He went to bed, telling everyone not to worry – he'd be as right as rain in the morning.

But next morning, he could not get out of bed without his legs collapsing under him. And within three days, he couldn't move any muscle from his chest downwards, and could hardly move his arms or work his fingers either.

He was rushed to hospital, but the doctors were baffled. Finally a specialist from Boston was sent for, and he spelled out the terrifying truth. Roosevelt had polio.

This illness – its full name was poliomyelitis, or infantile paralysis – was very common in those days. (It has almost died out now, thanks to vaccination.) It most often struck babies and young children, but you could catch it at any age, and if you caught it badly, it could leave you completely paralysed for life.

It soon became clear that Roosevelt *had* caught it badly – which meant that he might never move any of those muscles again.

*   *   *

By all the laws of logic, that should have been the end of Franklin D. Roosevelt as a politician. As far

Anna, James and Elliott. Roosevelt was with the boys when he fell overboard, and with all three when he fought a forest fire. (BBC Hulton)

The house at Campobello, where Roosevelt and his family were living at the time of the icy dip. (Peter Newark's Western Americana)

as the public was concerned, he hadn't been much of one, anyway. The feeling that he was just a spineless 'Mr Nice Guy' had lost him millions of votes at the last election.

Yet Roosevelt's sunny nature was only one side of his extraordinary character.

He hated to say 'no' to anybody when he could say 'yes'; he loathed to ride roughshod over anybody's feelings, and so got the reputation for being a softie. But, as the people who were close to him when he was at the Navy Department discovered, whenever this 'softie' had hard decisions to take – even major decisions, affecting the whole future of the nation – he was apt to take them with a dash, recklessness and courage that even Cousin Teddy would have envied.

He took one of those decisions now. It was not

quite as quick as usual. It was reached, in fact, only after agonies of alternating hope and despair. But it was by far the biggest decision he had ever made.

He wasn't going to quit. Somehow he was going to find a way of going right on with his political career, no matter how long it took, no matter what the cost.

His son Franklin – eight years old at the time – remembers seeing his father being carried on a stretcher into an ambulance, a day or two after the paralysis had set in.

'His head was lower than his feet,' he wrote, 'but in spite of that, he managed to wave to me, and his whole face burst into a tremendous sunny smile. So I decided he couldn't be sick after all . . .'

What Franklin Junior had seen was, of course, partly an act put on by a courageous father to cheer up a small, terrified son. But it was also more than that.

It was the beginning of the incredible fight back.

5

 The Incredible Fight Back

For the next three years, Franklin Roosevelt – as he himself described it later – 'rolled in the gutter with death'. It was obvious that he couldn't stage a big return to politics while he was lying flat on his back. He had to get power into at least some of those muscles. But polio was still something of a mystery disease, and could be a killer. A lot of people thought he would be risking his life if he tried to experiment with moving about.

Sara Roosevelt wanted him to retire completely. After all, she was a millionairess. If he just took to his bed, she could provide him with servants and luxuries, and look after him for the rest of his life. And he would be safe: there'd be no risk of the illness getting worse.

Eleanor, on the other hand, supported her husband's fight – and more important, never doubted that he would win. Probably her background – her childhood fight against tragedies – helped her enormously here. She knew, from direct experience, what it meant to be 'tried by fire': to face desperate situations, and to come through. She was determined that Franklin should have a chance to do the same. To quote the famous journalist, John Gunther, who knew Eleanor personally: 'She would not give an inch to his illness.' When Sara wanted Roosevelt to be moved out to the country, Eleanor insisted that he should stay right in the middle of New York. When Sara wanted to ban all talk of politics, Eleanor never stopped making plans for Roosevelt's future career.

To quote John Gunther again:

'There was a battle to the finish between these two remarkable women . . . Harsh words were seldom spoken; the intensity burned beneath the surface; the struggle was fierce just the same.'

Eleanor had one very important ally. A rising young politician called Louis Howe, who had been

The faithful friend – Roosevelt with Louis Howe, the man who gave up his own career to help Roosevelt stage a comeback. (Peter Newark's Western Americana)

an assistant to Roosevelt in his Navy Department days, instantly decided to give up everything and devote his life to helping his old boss. He came and moved in with the Roosevelts, and immediately started a big campaign to keep the name of F.D.R. before the public. On the very day that Roosevelt was first taken to hospital, and was actually lying totally helpless, Howe was sending out friendly letters in his name, congratulating various Democrat politicians who happened to have won some elections. Starting from that moment, people across America who had written off Franklin D. Roosevelt hurriedly began to think again!

Gradually, inch by inch, Roosevelt's muscles began to recover. First he got back the use of his arms and fingers. Then the big muscles on his back began to function, and he discovered that he could crawl, baby-like, across the floor. Ninety-nine men out of a hundred would have done these crawling experiments secretly, fearful of looking like a fool. Roosevelt invited Eleanor and the children in to watch and cheer him on, and made the whole thing a joke, a kind of family game. Before long, they were all watching him climbing up the stairs. He would clutch hold of the banisters, one by one, and haul himself up by his hands from step to step, giving a cheerful running commentary on his own performance as he went.

Then, once again, water played a part in the Roosevelt destiny – and this time, it had a healing role. Roosevelt heard that there was a dilapidated hotel in Georgia, which overlooked a small hot water lake called Warm Springs; and that bathing in this lake was said to help polio sufferers. (Weak muscles work very much better when they are buoyed up by water.) Roosevelt went down to Warm Springs for six weeks, and had himself taken into the pool every day. He felt life in his toes, he said, for the first time in three years.

After that, he revisited Warm Springs constantly, and rented a nearby house. A score or more of other polio sufferers started coming down to Warm Springs whenever Roosevelt was there. He called them his 'patients' or 'gang' and they treated him almost like a doctor. Day after day, he and his 'gang' would splash about in the warm water, usually doing exercises that Roosevelt had invented. You could almost say that the whole group of them were pioneering their own polio cure.

The atmosphere was – as usual with Roosevelt – sunny. There was a great deal of whooping and hollering and horsing about; everything was made to seem a kind of game; but, most important, under Roosevelt's leadership, his 'patients'' confidence kept growing, and their paralysed muscles seemed to respond and get better all the time. Roosevelt's own confidence was growing rapidly, too. Before long he built a house of his own beside Warm Springs, and gave it a most significant name: *The Little White House.*

It was at Warm Springs that people first noticed that a big change had come over Franklin D. Roosevelt. No one was ever to take him again for a mild, colourless 'Mr Nice Guy'. There was a radiant optimism about him which, from then onwards, made him the centre of attention everywhere he went. He had rolled in the gutter with death and come out winning. Nothing could stop him now.

47

Roosevelt had not, in fact, wholly recovered from polio. Once out of the water, he was never able to walk without crutches or someone's arm to lean on. And he would always be tied to a wheelchair. But everything else he could do as well as any other man, and one thing he could do better than almost any other man in the world: inspire *confidence*.

It was a quality that was shortly to be desperately needed. For a few years later, the whole of the United States was to find itself paralysed – not by polio, but by fear.

*   *   *

In 1924, Roosevelt was asked to make a political speech – which would mean his first appearance in public since he had become ill, three years before.

It wasn't to be a short speech either. An old friend, Al Smith, intended to stand as the Democratic candidate at the next Presidential election, and wanted Roosevelt to nominate him – which would mean speaking to thousands at Madison Square Garden, one of the largest halls in New York.

Typically, Roosevelt agreed without hesitation, and with hardly a thought about what a task he was undertaking.

He had to be pushed up to the platform in a wheelchair. Then he had to swing his way on crutches across the stage until he reached the speaker's desk. Once there, he had to lean on the desk all the time he was talking. But from the moment he began, the whole audience was mesmerised by the power of the new Franklin D. Roosevelt.

*Back in politics –
Roosevelt as
Governor of New
York, with the
Lt-Governor. This
photograph shows
the leg braces which
Roosevelt had to
wear after his
illness. Later, things
like that were kept
out of photographs,
because he wanted
the public to forget
that he was a
cripple.* (Oliver
Yates Collection)

Franklin D. Roosevelt

Using a quotation from a poem by Wordsworth that had once been a pet phrase of Cousin Teddy's, Roosevelt called Al Smith 'the Happy Warrior of the political battlefield'. But it was Roosevelt the audience thought of as a happy warrior. When he finished, they cheered him without stopping for an incredible *one hour and thirteen minutes* – and would have gone on for another hour if he hadn't quietened them by raising his hand.

It was one of the most tumultuous receptions in the history of U.S. politics. A commentator said: 'Adversity has made him the one leader commanding the respect of all sections of the land . . .'

From that day, Roosevelt was not only back in politics: he was a major political force, almost as big a national hero as Teddy had been in his heyday.

Before long, he was asked to stand as Governor of New York, regarded by many as the second most important position in the United States after the Presidency itself.

Roosevelt wanted a year or so more of exercising in Warm Springs, in the hope that he would be able to walk without crutches. But he discovered that he had beaten polio as far as it could be beaten, and so accepted the offer.

He was elected Governor of New York in 1928, the year that a certain Herbert Hoover became President of the U.S.A., and the nation began a downward slide towards financial collapse, the Great Depression, unemployment on a scale that it had never known . . . and terror.

6

 # A Nation in Terror

To this day, nobody fully understands what happened to the United States in October, 1929. It was as though the whole nation had been struck, out of the blue, by a paralysing illness, which became known as the Great Depression.

Just fourteen months before, the newly-elected President, Herbert Hoover, had been saying proudly that no nation in history had ever been so prosperous – so close, as he put it, to 'the final triumph over poverty'. And most Americans at that time would have agreed with him.

American factories poured out more goods – particularly modern luxuries, like cars and the recently-invented radios – than those of any other country on earth. Thanks to brilliantly reckless business men like Henry Ford (of motor car fame), the U.S.A. was pioneering mass-production methods that were the envy of the rest of the world.

But it is useless for factories to pour out goods if there is no one to pay for them, and pointless for cars to stream off assembly-lines if there are no customers in the showrooms waiting to buy. And after October, 1929, that began to be the situation, throughout the U.S.A.

The centre of the nation's financial world was Wall Street, New York, the exchange where stocks

Herbert Hoover – the President everyone blamed for the Depression. (Peter Newark's Western Americana)

and shares were daily bought and sold. Wall Street had always been a highly excitable place. One day, the market would be what was called 'bullish' – and the value of shares would rise so fast that fortunes would be made in a flash. On another day, conditions would be 'bearish': in other words, the value of shares would be falling, sometimes so dramatically that thousands of people would find themselves ruined in the course of a few hours.

In the early part of 1929, Wall Street had been a 'bull' market, with shares rising fast for day after day, week after week. People began to have a sneaking fear that this was too good to last. Suddenly, without anybody being able to put a finger on the cause, that sneaking fear turned into outright hysteria, and on October 29, 1929, an extraordinary situation arose. So few people wanted to buy shares that the whole stock market collapsed – or, as the papers put it, 'Wall Street crashed'. Shares went

The Wall Street Crash – this rare photograph actually shows the stockbrokers panicking on the day in October, 1929, when the Stock Exchange collapsed, bringing ruin and poverty to thousands. (Peter Newark's Western Americana)

down by millions of dollars overnight, wiping out not only the fortunes of rich families, but the nest-eggs of hundreds and thousands of small savers, too. A nationwide panic set in. People rushed to their banks to draw out what money they had left. The banks simply could not cope with so many un-expected demands, and began to close in their thousands. Eventually, a third of all the banks in the United States closed their doors; and people who had money in those banks simply lost it! The panic spread rapidly to businesses, which cut their losses the obvious way, by lowering wages and dismissing staff. Wages throughout the U.S. dropped by nearly half (40%). Unemployment leapt to a staggering total. Estimates vary, but in the end the figure may well have been as high as 17,000,000 – which meant that one quarter of all the workers were without jobs.

Soon the panic spread out across the world. Since the U.S. could no longer buy wheat from Canada, the Canadians found themselves having to burn it by the ton. The Brazilians found they had to do the same with their coffee beans. In Europe, a sudden slump hit one country after another. Britain faced the highest unemployment in its history. In Germany, money became almost totally valueless, and at one point, even a wheelbarrow full of mark notes was not enough to buy a square meal for a family. The Germans became so frightened that they turned to the strongest man they could find to lead them – and voted for Adolf Hitler.

Americans were not quite in such straits; but for increasing numbers of them, things were looking really desperate.

Hundreds and thousands of people hadn't the money to pay the mortgages on their houses, and were turned out of their homes. They included people from every part of society. Doctors, lawyers, artists, shop owners, farmers – anyone who had a job to lose or a business that could go bankrupt was in danger of finding himself suddenly without a cent in his pocket or a roof over his head. In one town, the homeless included two families who were so well-known locally that they had actually had streets named after them! Not that that is much consolation when you are walking the pavements, penniless.

More than a million Americans were now doing just that. They formed a vast 'vagabond army', as it was called, wandering desolately from town to town searching for any opportunity to earn, beg or steal the means to keep alive. They slept at night under the stars – or headed for the nearest railway station to creep into railway carriages or goods wagons, where they could at least get some shelter if it rained. The South Pacific Railroad turned 683,000 trespassers off their trains in a single year. Then the company took pity on the vagabonds, and began arranging for extra carriages to be available for them to sleep in!

Other destitute people built shanty towns, out of odd bits of wood and pieces of rusty corrugated iron, on the edges of the big cities. They called these towns 'Hoovervilles', after the President whom they believed had got the country into this mess, and was doing nothing to help them. Hoover became the most hated man in America. An empty pocket turned inside out (a sign that its owner hadn't a cent in the world) became known as a 'Hoover flag'. One

A Hooverville – someone desperately tries to sell apples outside one of the shanty towns built by the homeless. (Peter Newark's Western Americana)

Hundreds of unemployed people standing in a 'breadline' for a free handout of soup and food. (Peter Newark's Western Americana)

enterprising hitch-hiker, it was said, travelled the thousands of miles from New York to California by hanging a notice round his neck threatening: 'Give me a lift or I'll vote for Hoover!'

One unemployed man in Baltimore was photographed with a still more startling notice round his neck:

I AM FOR SALE.
I must have work or starve.
Your inquiry appreciated.

His simple, bleak message summed up the plight of a quarter of the United States. And the statement 'I must have work or starve' was not much of an

57

exaggeration. In those days to be workless did literally mean to face starvation. Long queues formed wherever the Salvation Army or any other charity organisation handed out soup and food (usually not more than a slice or two of bread). The people in the queues were called the 'breadliners' – and there were soon millions of them.

To understand the misery, bewilderment and bitterness of the time, you only have to listen to the words of the popular hit song of the period – 'Buddy, Can You Spare a Dime?'

There was one place in America where the jobless were *not* being treated as dirt or as 'men for sale'. Curiously enough, it was the place where the whole tragic panic had begun – New York.

In this state, and this state alone, unemployment pay was being handed out automatically to residents who couldn't find work. In addition, huge sums were set aside to help feed and clothe the destitute and starving thousands who poured into New York from around the country. It wasn't left to charities to feed the breadliners.

All these ideas – including unemployment pay, which was entirely new to America – had been introduced by New York's recently-elected governor, the one U.S. politician who not only felt for the unemployed, but acted fast and decisively to help them: Franklin D. Roosevelt.

*   *   *

Roosevelt, in other words, was at last fulfilling his old, old dream of fighting on behalf of the poor. The state, he said flatly, owed all men and women the chance to earn a living, and should give them enough to buy the necessities of life even if it couldn't give them work. (He applied this even to people over working age, and gave New York the U.S.A.'s first Old Age Pension scheme, too.)

This belief – accepted by almost every Western nation now – was unheard-of in the U.S. in those days. Some people called it wild and dangerous talk. But not the people of New York. Although Roosevelt's schemes cost them a fortune in rates, that seemed a small price to pay for making their state a haven of hope in a country gone mad.

Roosevelt had originally been elected by 25,000 votes. Two years later, when there was another election, he was returned to office by a staggering vote of 750,000 – by far the largest majority in the history of New York.

Hoover, meanwhile, was continuing to make himself the most hated man in the country. He believed in spending money to help banks and big corporations, in the hope that this would lead to more people being offered jobs; but he stubbornly refused to consider giving government cash directly to the victims of the Depression. Hundreds of unemployed veteran soldiers arrived in Washington, camping out in a Hooverville on the outskirts of the city, to stage a protest on the very doorstep of the White House. Hoover called out the army, and under General Douglas MacArthur (who later became famous in World War II), the pathetic shanty town was attacked by four troops of cavalry, four of infantry, a machine-gun squadron and six tanks! The ramshackle wooden huts were burned to the ground, and all the veterans could do was go back to their lives of hopeless wandering and queueing up in breadlines. And there were men amongst them who had been war heroes just fourteen years before.

A few months later there was a Presidential election. The Democrats, remembering Roosevelt's extraordinary success as Governor of New York, chose him as their candidate against Hoover.

It was the first time in history that anyone had fought a Presidential campaign from a wheelchair, but Roosevelt was not in the least worried. 'When you have spent two years in bed trying to wiggle your big toe, everything else seems easy,' he remarked, and, in fact, his sunny confidence came across so strongly that during the campaign, most people entirely forgot that he *was* an invalid.

Certainly, Roosevelt took care not to remind them. Whenever he was photographed for the newspapers, sticks, crutches and wheelchairs were kept well out of sight. He usually appeared standing, waving a large hat, sporting a cigarette in an extremely long holder (the fashion of the day), and grinning as if he hadn't a care in the world – and no one else needed to have one either! Wherever he went, he promised everyone, rich or poor, in work or out of it, a 'New Deal'. And just to emphasise the point, he had the bands play a defiant 'Happy Days Are Here Again'.

Never in history had Americans needed a new deal more desperately, and it isn't surprising that Roosevelt won by a large majority.

*   *   *

In the U.S., a new President does not take over

power immediately. He has to wait until what is called his 'Inauguration' early in the following year.

Roosevelt, then, did not actually become President of the United States until March, 1932. And in the months between his election and the inauguration, the nation's crisis suddenly deepened into total chaos.

A third of the banks had already closed down, as we have seen. Now the remaining ones were finding it impossible to stay open. People were drawing out their savings at such a hysterical rate that in every Main Street banks were bolting their doors to stop themselves going bust. All farming came to a halt; no one had money to pay for the farmers' produce. In the huge manufacturing city of Detroit, centre of the car industry, all the factories shut down because the automobile companies did not have the means to pay their workers for even one more week!

Fathers of families were going over refuse heaps and hunting through dustbins to find something – anything – for their children to eat. It was believed that civil war, or revolution, would break out at any minute. Perhaps democracy was a failure, people said. Perhaps the U.S.A., like Germany, needed a Hitler to take command and put things right. Or perhaps Communism was the only answer . . .

The panic grew and grew, and fights began to break out between the police and the unemployed. Roosevelt himself was the target of a mad gunman, just as Cousin Teddy had been. But Roosevelt was luckier. A woman standing behind the gunman jogged his arm just as he was taking aim, and the bullets hit, not Roosevelt, but the man to whom he happened to be chatting, the Mayor of Chicago.

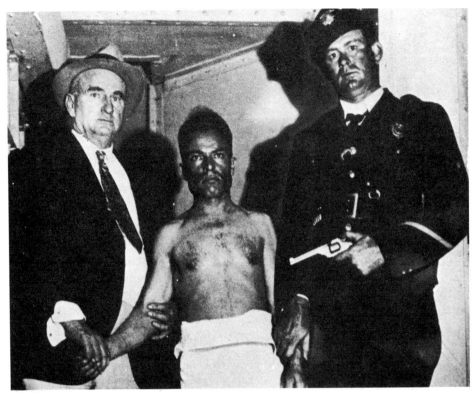

The madman who fired at Roosevelt, but hit and killed the Mayor of Chicago. He has just been stripped and searched. (Peter Newark's Western Americana)

The police wanted to hurry Roosevelt off to safety, but he flatly refused to go. Instead, he insisted on taking the wounded Mayor to hospital in his own car. Not only that, but Roosevelt stayed beside the injured man, holding him still and trying to calm him, all the way.

Just a month later, he was facing the infinitely more difficult task of trying to calm his country.

On March 4, his actual inauguration day, the nation's whole financial system seized up. Not a bank was able to open throughout the length and breadth of the United States. Wall Street, for the first time in its turbulent history, simply stopped trading – and the whole Stock Exchange closed down.

Everybody's money was now out of reach. *Everybody's* job was in extreme danger. *Every* business was facing collapse.

In a state not so much of panic now, but of hushed, numbed horror, the people clustered round their radios to hear their brand-new President speak.

They expected, perhaps, a torrent of political ranting and raving. Instead, they heard a cheerful, fatherly voice reminding them that the fields were still there; the factories were still there; abundance was still at the door, and there was no logical reason why the United States should not become, once again, the most prosperous nation on earth.

'Let me assert my firm belief,' said Roosevelt, 'that the only thing we have to fear is fear itself – nameless, unreasoning, unjustified terror.'

'The only thing we have to fear is fear . . .' It was the most famous line that Roosevelt ever spoke – and the moment he'd said it, a long-unfamiliar feeling began to sweep across the nation.

People found themselves turning to each other and actually smiling – because suddenly, unbelievably, *confidence* was in the air.

7

 The Rescue

Roosevelt's first action as President was entirely typical.

Seeing that all the banks had closed down, the most sensible course, it seemed to him, was to make a joke of the whole thing – and declare a national bank holiday!

It was a pretty strange bank holiday, because it was really a *money* holiday too. The most popular film of the time – *King Kong* – played to empty cinemas, because nobody had any dollars or cents to buy tickets. In New Orleans, a big race meeting packed up half-time because nobody could place any bets. At Madison Square Garden, where a boxing semi-final was being held, the promoters had the bright idea of taking goods at the box office instead of cash. They collected a weird collection of objects, from sparking plugs to jigsaw puzzles, but at least they got a crowd in to see the sport!

The bank holiday over, Roosevelt set to work – and during the next hundred days, to quote John Gunther, 'did more to change American life than anyone else had done in a hundred years.'

He had always had a talent for making quick decisions; for quietly acting while everybody else was talking. Now that talent was put to use with a vengeance.

Bill after bill poured out of the White House, and Congress was so pleased to see action – *any* kind of action – being taken, that it passed them all, very often the same day.

The Government was to have absolute powers over banking and foreign exchange, and could seize all the gold in the country if it desired. Banks would reopen under Government supervision, to make sure they didn't close their doors to the public again. Prohibition – the ban on the sale of alcoholic drink, which had caused the rise of the Chicago gangsters a few years earlier – was abolished. A Civilian Conservation Corps was set up to provide work for teenagers on the breadlines. An agricultural aid scheme was introduced to provide government

On his first Sunday in the White House, at one of the gravest times of crisis in US history, Roosevelt and his family set off for church. (Peter Newark's Western Americana)

money to farmers, in return for growing certain crops. A Home Owners Loan Corporation was set up to help people buy houses again, and get them home from the Hoovervilles. Congress gave Roosevelt a mind-boggling $3,300,000,000 to be spent on new schools, new town halls, new railways and new houses to replace slums throughout the country. (Roosevelt had never forgotten that sickening moment when he had first sighted a slum.) This was the largest rebuilding programme ever thought of in any country's history, and would give literally millions of jobs to the unemployed. Long-term schemes were also started to bring the United States into the new age of electricity by building dams and power-stations on an enormous scale. In the Tennessee Valley, for example, only two farms out of every hundred had electric light. Roosevelt set up a Tennessee Valley Authority with powers to change the whole area, harnessing the waters of a wild, torrential river for the benefit of seven states. An Industrial Recovery Act was passed, which gave workers the chance to form big trade unions, and fight for a decent minimum wage. New controls were brought in to stop reckless speculation, and put paid to the old, crazy Wall Street. And finally, on the last of the hundred days, a bill was passed which guaranteed everybody's bank account – so that if ever a bank went bust again, the Government would see to it that no customer lost a penny.

This was Roosevelt's 'New Deal' for the United States – and there was, in fact, a great deal that was new about it. For the first time, the government was looking after the wellbeing of the poorest citizen no matter what it cost the well-to-do. But, in

A New Deal for workers. Roosevelt's schemes brought unemployment down from 17,000,000 to 10,000,000 – almost overnight! (Peter Newark's Western Americana)

Roosevelt's opinion, everyone benefited. Because they had more money, the poor could buy more products; factories reopened, farms came back to life – and hence more profit went into the pockets of the well-to-do! Roosevelt spent money recklessly, in the belief that the more he spent, the more money there would be back in circulation; and on the whole, the system worked. It swept America rapidly out of the worst of the depression. It brought unemployment down from seventeen to ten million, and then to eight million. And it totally changed the mood of the country, which became once again the buoyant, confident U.S.A., building faster, progressing faster, than any nation on earth.

It would be wrong to pretend, though, that everything became perfect. The Hoovervilles and the breadlines disappeared: people's life savings became safe: workers all over America had new hope, and a lot of them – at last – actually had work! But unemployment stubbornly refused to drop below 8,000,000 – and suddenly a new disaster brought poverty and hunger to millions in six southern American states: Kansas, Nebraska, New Mexico, Colorado, Oklahoma and Texas.

This disaster was really Nature taking her revenge for the greediness of farmers. For twenty years or more, they had been ploughing up the vast American prairies to grow the very maximum of wheat, or grazing them with so much cattle that there was hardly a blade of grass, or a tree, to be seen for miles and miles. But in that part of the world, the soil is very thin, and if no grass is allowed to grow on it, and there are no tree-roots to bind it and hold it down, it is liable to turn into dust the first time there is a bad drought.

The drought came in 1932. By late 1933, there had been hardly any rain in the area for eighteen months – and suddenly, with all the speed and horror of a disaster movie, great dust storms blew up all the way from Oklahoma to South Dakota. The skies turned pitch-black with the swirling dust, and

Bad times for the South. Great dust storms turned farms into deserts across six states. (Peter Newark's Western Americana)

the winds blew away the topsoil at the rate of 300 million tons a day. One old farmer wryly remarked that he could look out of his window and count the Kansas farms flying past – and he wasn't exaggerating much. When the soil took off, the farms were literally blown sky-high with it. Nothing was left but dusty sand which buried the farmhouses and choked the lungs – desert sand in which not a single thing would grow.

All the farmers could do was pack up their belongings, pile into their battered cars and move away from what was now known as The Great Dust Bowl. The roads to California were lined with decrepit 1925 Dodges and 1923 Model-T Fords, into each of which would be squeezed not only a whole family, but mattresses, suitcases, saucepans, jugs – everything that the family needed to live on! There were so many of these refugees from Nature that it was impossible to find work for them all to do. But at least there was now a U.S. government that *cared*. Roosevelt set up a Farm Administration that was at one time feeding and supporting 30,000 families in California alone.

*   *   *

In 1936, Roosevelt stood again as President, and it was suddenly clear that he had made powerful enemies. His policy of spending huge sums to help the poor had, of course, meant high taxes for the rich – and the rich were very far from pleased. (Although there were exceptions. One Boston merchant, who was having to give half his income every year in taxes, said publicly: 'When I see what my country is getting for its money now, I consider my taxpaying to be the best bargain of my life.')

The fact that Roosevelt had allowed the workers to get organised into big trade unions frightened managements. The judges in the American Supreme Court had actually reversed some of his New Deal laws, declaring them illegal. And some leading members of his own Democratic party now turned against him, believing that he was leading the U.S. towards communism. Others were scared that all the billions of dollars he was spending would make the country bankrupt – although the prosperity it was creating was now obvious, everywhere one looked. National production had risen 67% since Roosevelt had taken over, and many businesses simply could not cope with the flood of new orders.

During the election, Roosevelt was attacked by the majority of big businessmen – and by 80% of the newspapers, which, of course, the businessmen owned. Not that he was worried in the least. The mild Roosevelt, who used to leave the room to avoid unpleasant scenes, had gone for ever. And although his nature was still basically sunny, the new Roosevelt was perfectly capable of making stormy speeches, if the occasion demanded it. He *welcomed* the hatred of the rich, he said contemptuously – and warned that if he was re-elected, he would spend more money, to help more people, than ever.

The ordinary men and women of America knew who their friend was. Totally ignoring the news-papers, and the angry bellows from the business world, they returned Roosevelt with one of the biggest landslide majorities in the history of American elections. True to his promise, he im-mediately went on to give the whole of the U.S.A. unemployment relief and Old Age Pensions, so that no American would ever be wholly destitute, or be left to face starvation, again.

The rich were horrified – but his popularity with the general public now knew no bounds. Poor people would come up to him in the street and touch him as though he were a Pope or a saint. One newspaper remarked: 'If Roosevelt were to say a kind word for the man-eating shark, people would look thoughtful and say perhaps there *are* two sides to the question.'

Certainly, never before had the American public as a whole felt such an extraordinary warmth towards their President. Partly, of course, this was because Roosevelt, almost single-handed, had saved them from the dark days of terror. But there were other reasons, too. Roosevelt's sunny nature – considered a sign of weakness all through his early years – gave him a natural instinct for dealing with the man in the street. For example, he was the first politician who really understood how to use that new invention, radio. Other politicians would roar their speeches into the microphone as if they were addressing a national rally. Roosevelt made the announcer say that the President wanted his listeners to feel he had dropped in for a fireside chat. By the late 1930s, these fireside chats had made Roosevelt's voice as cosily familiar to millions of radio listeners as those of Bob Hope or Bing Crosby.

Eleanor Roosevelt also played a part in making the President seem less aloof and remote. During Roosevelt's first term, she had tirelessly travelled up and down the country, acting as the President's eyes and ears. At the height of the Depression, she would turn up all over the place – one day queuing in a breadline, the next chatting to the folk in a Hooverville, the next looking into conditions at a Negro school. A famous cartoon appeared in the *New Yorker*, showing two men in the depths of a coalmine, one saying to the other: 'For gosh sakes, here comes Mrs Roosevelt!' A popular joke going the rounds concerned the famous explorer Admiral Byrd, setting two places for dinner in his Antarctic shack, 'just in case Eleanor drops in'.

In 1936, just before Roosevelt had become President for the second time, Mrs Roosevelt suddenly added journalism to all her other activities. She started a column which appeared in newspapers all over the country, describing in detail her daily life as First Lady of America. With Franklin chatting on the radio every few months, and Eleanor's column taking them into the White House day by day, the Americans came to regard the Roosevelts almost as next-door neighbours, if not personal friends.

Eleanor did not confide all her troubles to her readers. She made no mention, for instance, of the financial difficulties of running the White House. It was estimated to have cost her $150,000 a week, whereas Roosevelt's Presidential salary was only $5000 a week. It was a good job that Sara Roosevelt was in the background, with her millions, to lend a hand.

Left: *Roosevelt as the 1930s cartoonist saw him, complete with three FDR trade-marks: the long cigarette-holder, the jutting jaw, and the Depression defying grin . . .* (Wide World Photos)

Right: *. . . an actual cartoon – without the cigarette-holder!* (Oliver Yates Collection)

The rescuer of America – President Franklin D. Roosevelt, at the height of his popularity in the late 1930s. (BBC Hulton)

Important visitors – the Roosevelts entertain the King and Queen of England. Left to right: Eleanor Roosevelt, King George VI, Sara Roosevelt, Queen Elizabeth and Roosevelt. (Oliver Yates Collection)

Sara and Eleanor were no longer at daggers drawn. Sara – now an old lady of almost eighty – was delighted at her son's astonishingly good health, and overjoyed that he had become President. She was the first woman ever to see her son in the White House. 'Of course,' she told everybody, 'I'd always planned it that way.' She was still a commanding mother. She once snapped to a reporter: 'Of course Franklin isn't going to church tomorrow. The naughty boy's got behind with answering his mail.'

Sara was not always generous with her millions. She had a habit of quarrelling endlessly over tradesmen's bills. During Roosevelt's second term as President, America became a more important power in the eyes of the world than ever before, and European heads of state were always coming on visits. In 1939, they included King George VI and Queen Elizabeth of England, who were to stay for a while at the Roosevelts' country home.

75

The story goes that Sara had all the toilets re-plumbed specially for the occasion, but after the Royal visit was over, refused to pay the plumber's bill. The plumber came and took away everything he'd installed, and next day, a toilet seat was on show in the window of the shop, labelled: 'The King and Queen sat here.'

Even Sara Roosevelt paid up rather promptly after that.

*　　*　　*

Roosevelt, then, had won his battle to rescue the U.S.A. But now, and for the rest of his life, he was to be involved in a still more titanic struggle.

Starting slowly, and seeming to do nothing much at first, he ended by playing a bigger part than any other man in rescuing the *world* – from perhaps the darkest tyranny that it had ever known.

8

 War in
Europe

By the time Roosevelt was a year into his second
term as President (1937–41), it was obvious to him
that the world was rushing headlong towards war.

The trouble began in Europe, where the Depression
that had ravaged the U.S. had brought total collapse
to Germany. As we have seen, at almost the same
time that the Americans were turning to Roosevelt,
the Germans had turned to a man whose message
had been very different: who had offered the people
strength through a mixture of iron discipline, hate
and fear.

In 1933, Adolf Hitler had demanded, and obtained,
from the German parliament, the Reichstag, very
similar powers to those which Roosevelt had been
given by Congress: control of the country's money,
and permission to take emergency action of almost
any kind to save the nation. But Hitler had used
those powers to crush all opposition, to set up a reign
of terror, and to build a massive army and air force
with which he planned to conquer the whole of
Europe – although very few people outside Germany
believed he would actually make the attempt.

Only one European statesman – Winston Churchill,
then a backbench M.P. – continually warned the
world what Hitler was planning to do.

Roosevelt read Churchill's speeches, and found he

agreed with them. He also began to feel a warm admiration for this Englishman who spoke out so boldly. He felt an urge to help; but the last thing the U.S. wanted to do was tangle in Europe's affairs, and even to suggest it would have been political suicide. A very determined Congress had just insisted on passing a Neutrality Law, saying that if a war broke out anywhere in the world, the U.S. would not give any kind of help to either side.

The world scene continued to darken, until everything looked as black as a Kansas sky at the height of a dust storm.

In 1935 the Italian dictator Mussolini, a personal friend of Hitler, marched an army into the peaceful neighbouring country of Abyssinia. In 1936 another Hitler admirer, General Franco, attempted to seize power in Spain, and started a bitter civil war. In 1937, the war threat became literally worldwide. The Japanese, who were soon to become close allies of Hitler and Mussolini, marched into China, beginning a struggle to conquer that vast country that was to continue for year after year. This was exceptionally embarrassing to Roosevelt, because Japan was receiving large supplies of American oil and scrap metal at the time. He would certainly have liked to have cut off those supplies without more ado. But while Japan was receiving them, it was safe to say that she would not declare war on the U.S., whereas if they were stopped, she might. Roosevelt was not at all anxious to plunge an unwilling and unprepared U.S. into war. He compromised, rather weakly, by sending some ships and guns to China. All this was against Congress's Neutrality Act, of course, but because war hadn't

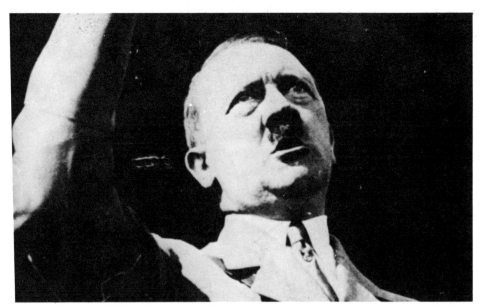

Adolf Hitler, the German dictator who launched the whole world into war.
(Peter Newark's Historical Pictures)

actually been *declared* between Japan and China, it could be said not to apply.

In 1938, Hitler himself began to move. Germany seized Austria overnight, and threatened to march into Czechoslovakia. Britain's Prime Minister, Neville Chamberlain, flew to see Hitler and (to Winston Churchill's horror) signed a treaty allowing the German dictator to take some of Czechoslovakia, provided he promised not to attack any more countries. The British people cheered themselves hoarse at the thought that there wouldn't be a war; and the U.S. public cheered almost as loudly. Roosevelt tried to get Congress to change the Neutrality Act, but it wouldn't listen. He also sent requests to Hitler and Mussolini for promises that they weren't intending to make war on any other nation, but neither dictator even bothered to reply!

In 1939 Hitler, convinced that Britain would not

fight and that the U.S. would not interfere (or, perhaps, too power-drunk to care if they did), seized more of Czechoslovakia and marched into Poland. Britain and France immediately declared war.

It is possible that, secretly, Roosevelt would have liked to have done the same. But he was President of a nation that still passionately wanted to steer clear of the war, and it had never been his way to block what he believed to be the will of the people.

He broadcast a fireside chat promising that if it was in his power to prevent it, there would be no 'blackout of peace' for Americans.

Nothing, though, could stop him taking sides. In the same broadcast he said that in the face of the Hitler peril, no one had to be 'neutral in thought'. Perhaps, as at the beginning of World War I, he 'just knew' he was going to do some 'awful unneutral thing' before he was through. In fact, he started being distinctly unneutral almost at once.

Within a few hours of declaring war, the British Prime Minister, Neville Chamberlain, appointed Winston Churchill to be the First Lord of the Admiralty. In other words, Churchill was now doing virtually the same job for Britain that Roosevelt had done for America in World War I. Surely that meant that there was some kind of bond between them, Roosevelt thought; and on a sudden impulse, he calmly telephoned Churchill in London and introduced himself. (That first meeting, in 1918, had been long forgotten.)

The telephone call was typical of Roosevelt – a casual, friendly, informal assurance of friendship from the other side of the world, at the moment when it was most needed.

He followed it up with a letter, in which he said:

'I shall at all times welcome it if you will keep me in touch personally with anything you want me to know about . . .'

When Churchill read this letter, he could hardly believe his eyes. Here was the President of the United States, the most powerful country on earth, telling him that he would whisper anything he wanted directly into his ear!

Churchill seized the opportunity with relish. From then onwards, he and Roosevelt exchanged a constant stream of letters, messages and telegrams – so that Roosevelt, in faraway Washington, was kept in almost as close touch with Britain's problems as a member of the British cabinet.

More than that, day in and day out, Roosevelt was wide open to all the Churchillian arguments about why Hitler must be beaten and how, with American help, this could be done.

And Churchill, on the subject of defeating Hitler, was perhaps the most persuasive arguer in history.

*   *   *

Winston Churchill was not the only significant person to catch the President's ear during the first months of World War II.

On 11th October, 1939 – barely five weeks after the war had begun – Roosevelt had a visit from a very colourful character, an eccentric amateur scientist called Dr Alexander Sachs.

Dr Sachs was worried about rumours he had heard. Hitler's scientists were said to be experimenting with something he called 'Instantaneous

'No one has to be neutral in thought.' A grim Roosevelt broadcasting in 1940.
(BBC Hulton)

Emissions of Fast Neutrons in the Interaction of
Slow Neutrons with Uranium.' He had with him a
letter from Albert Einstein, the greatest scientist of
the twentieth century, who was now in the U.S.
Einstein's letter confirmed the rumours, and tried to
explain how worrying they were.

Roosevelt quite obviously did not understand a
word that his visitor was saying, or what Albert
Einstein had written.

He looked so bored that Dr Sachs suddenly broke
off, and said:

'Look, Mr President. I've had to pay my train fare to Washington, and it's cost me a lot of money which I can't get back from the Income Tax. So will you *please* pay attention?'

Roosevelt, with an apologetic grin, pulled himself together and listened patiently while Dr Sachs read aloud a very long memorandum. He could still only understand about one word in every ten, but suddenly the purpose of all this dawned on him.

'What you're after, Alex,' he said slowly, 'is to see that these Nazis don't blow us up.'

Dr Sachs nodded. At last the message had got through.

'Precisely, Mr President.'

'Right,' said Roosevelt. 'This requires action.'

He reached for the telephone, and gave a few casual instructions. Within days, a small organisation had been set up to inquire into nuclear fission. Eventually it grew into a vast enterprise costing two billion dollars – but Roosevelt was always ready to spend money like water, if he thought the American people were in danger.

Five years later, that organisation, with British help, evolved the atom bomb.

It's a strange thought that that development – the most solemn and terrifying in the story of the human race – might never have happened but for one very small thing.

This was Dr Alexander Sachs' remarkable ability to make the President sit up and listen, even though he couldn't grasp a word of what was being said.

9

 'Keep Britain Afloat'

Churchill, sending his constant stream of messages from faraway Britain, did not just make the President sit up. Step by step, as he read the messages and answered them, Roosevelt found that he and Churchill were becoming close associates – even personal friends.

From Roosevelt's point of view, Churchill must have seemed a crazy, bewildering mixture of himself and Cousin Teddy. Like Roosevelt, Churchill came from a rich political family – his father, Lord Randolph Churchill, had been Chancellor of the Exchequer under Queen Victoria. Like Roosevelt, Churchill had tried to help the poor. In fact, with Lloyd George, he had started unemployment pay and Old Age Pensions in Britain a quarter of a century before Roosevelt had introduced them in America. Again like Roosevelt, he had been in charge of a navy during the First World War.

But there the resemblance between Churchill and *Franklin* Roosevelt ended. Churchill had had anything but a serene childhood – he had been publicly flogged at school from the age of eight, and was an exceptionally troublesome boy. Whereas Roosevelt had been stopped by his father from joining the Navy, Churchill had been encouraged by Lord Randolph to join the Army; and Churchill's early life

– fighting in wars around the world, taking part in a death-or-glory cavalry charge, and becoming a national hero through his Boer War exploits – were reminiscent of Cousin Teddy at his wildest.

What was more, Winston Churchill also had a famous roar – which he was soon to use with devastating effect.

In April, 1940, Hitler seized Norway, and a month later, marched his armies into Holland, Belgium and France. A panicky Britain hurriedly made Churchill Prime Minister. Within less than a fortnight, Holland and Belgium had been overthrown and France itself was on the point of surrendering. The British army, which was on French soil, escaped only through the miracle of Dunkirk. Then Britain was alone, facing a Nazi-occupied Europe, with a seemingly unbeatable German army poised to strike just twenty miles away across the Channel.

Churchill's roar of defiance echoed round the world and shook even Adolf Hitler.

'We shall fight on the beaches. We shall fight on the landing grounds. We shall fight in the fields and in the streets. We shall *never* surrender . . .'

Almost immediately, the Battle of Britain began, with day after day, week after week of ferocious air battles between the Royal Air Force and the Luftwaffe, fought high up in the blue summer skies. With Churchillian reports straight from London piling on to his desk, Roosevelt felt almost as involved as if the battle was taking place over Washington.

The United States waited for the result of the battle with bated breath – but Roosevelt had had enough of waiting. Not caring whether or not it was the proper way for a neutral country to behave, he found a loophole in the Neutrality Act and began sending munitions to Britain. In September, 1940, in answer to a special appeal from Churchill, he sent fifty old U.S. destroyers. They were very battered and rusty ships, many of them from America's scrapyards; but they could float and they could fight, which was all that mattered.

That very month, the Battle of Britain ended with the defeat of the Luftwaffe. But then the blitzes began, bombs raining down on London and other cities every night. Many Americans doubted if Britain could take much more. Roosevelt's closest advisers had, in fact, been telling him ever since Dunkirk that Britain only had one chance in three of pulling through. Roosevelt just grinned and told them: 'Wait and see, boys. You just wait and see!' He knew, from his constant contact with Churchill, that there was no thought of defeat in the British Prime Minister's mind. One could almost say that Roosevelt had met his equal in the art of keeping confident when things looked black.

Roosevelt now faced a battle which required all the confidence that even he could muster. In November, 1940, there was another Presidential election – and Roosevelt, breaking one of the strictest unwritten laws of American politics, decided to stand for a third term. (Now it's a *written* law, and Presidents *have* to retire after two terms in the White House.) Even some of his closest supporters were horrified. Eight years in the White House – doing what many believe to be the most responsible and demanding job in the world – was considered to be enough for anyone. Twelve years would not only put a terrible strain on a man's health; it would affect his mind, make him arrogant like a dictator.

Roosevelt laughed at these theories – but even if they were true, he believed that he had no choice. He was in the middle of preparations to give Churchill more aid than ever before, and he knew this was vital if the free world was to be saved. He would be failing in his duty if he stepped down now, and allowed someone to take his place who would make America strictly neutral once more.

His Republican opponent, Wendell Wilkie, made a great point of Roosevelt's warlike policies. Roosevelt had just introduced peacetime conscription, calling up millions of men for the forces – and Wilkie solemnly warned the Americans that if they voted for Roosevelt, within five months the United States would be at war. This prompted Roosevelt to make a speech which many people have said was flagrantly dishonest. 'And while I am talking to you mothers and fathers,' he said, 'I will give you one more assurance. I have said this before, but I shall say it again and again and again. Your boys are not going to be sent into any foreign wars.'

Before he made the speech, his advisers told him that he ought to add the words: '. . . unless we are attacked.' Roosevelt said that they were quite un-necessary. 'Of course we'll fight if we're attacked. If somebody fights us, it isn't a *foreign* war, anyway. What do you want me to do? Guarantee that we'll only fight if there's another American Civil War?'

A reasonable argument – but it didn't alter the fact that the speech gave American parents the impression that Roosevelt was promising to keep their boys at home.

It was a promise that, a year and a month later, Roosevelt was very definitely unable to keep.

* * *

Roosevelt won the election – but this time, it wasn't with a landslide majority. Too many people were worried about what twelve years as President might do to a man. Other voters, desperate for peace, believed that the nation was being led, step by step, into war. And a few, like Colonel Lindbergh, the ace

A New York Times *announcing the result of the 1940 election. Roosevelt promised to keep America out of the war . . . but privately, he was already joining in!* (Peter Newark's Western Americana)

pilot who had been first to fly the Atlantic, came close to being actual supporters of Hitler. The war in Europe was as good as lost, they kept proclaiming. The United States was being deluded by Churchill's lies. The truth was that Britain was being blitzed out of existence, and would soon collapse.

As the winter of 1940–41 wore on, and every night British cities were blasted and turned into infernos of smoke and flame, even Roosevelt had a moment of anxiety. There was no doubting Churchill's determination. He had proof of it on his desk almost every day. But could he be sure that Churchill was carrying the British with him? Were the rumour-mongers right? Was Britain on the point of cracking up?

Roosevelt sent an old friend called Harry Hopkins over to London on an odd but historic mission. He was to assure Churchill personally that Roosevelt would go to all lengths short of war to help Britain. At the same time, he was to look around, talk to the people in the streets, and report back privately to Roosevelt on what he saw.

Churchill welcomed Hopkins with great courtesy – and equally great bewilderment. This American wasn't a war expert of any sort. All that was known about him was that he'd helped in a Roosevelt unemployment relief programme. Churchill assumed that for some reason Roosevelt was suddenly concerned about Britain's poor.

'We must – ah – plan a good life for the – ah – cottagers after the war,' he remarked politely, with a lordly wave of the famous Churchillian cigar.

Hopkins stared.

'I don't give a damn about cottagers. I'm here to

see what we can do about that fellow Hitler.'

Churchill brightened visibly.

'In that case, Mr Hopkins, come into the library,' he said and did not stop speaking about his plans for beating Hitler until 4 a.m.

Hopkins was impressed, but still doubtful. This Churchill could have been handing him a load of rubbish. But next day, he went out and about and started talking to the ordinary men and women of London. Most of them had been through nights of bombing, but none looked depressed or dismayed, and it had plainly not entered their heads that Hitler could win.

Hopkins had no doubts now. He rushed back to his hotel, and that very night wrote to Roosevelt: 'The people here are amazing, from Churchill down. But they need help desperately and I am sure you will permit nothing to stand in your way.'

Hopkins had told Roosevelt all that he needed to know. From that moment on, he had one main objective, more difficult perhaps even than the rescuing of the United States. At all costs, he had (as he put it) to 'keep Britain afloat.'

He had already had the Neutrality Act amended – and replaced by a revolutionary measure which only Roosevelt could have thought of, called 'Lease-Lend'. Under this, America agreed to *lend* any amount of arms to any country which the President thought needed support. Payment for them could be made later – if necessary, much later, after victory had been won. This arrangement allowed Roosevelt to pour out dollars unlimited, in the usual reckless Roosevelt manner, to make airplanes, tanks, ships and guns for sending direct to Britain, or any other

Harry Hopkins, Roosevelt's personal messenger, who went to talk to Churchill and send back a secret report on Britain. (Peter Newark's Western Americana)

country fighting Hitler. Curiously enough, this benefited America as much as it did Britain. Factories began working twenty-four hours a day, and at last there was no major unemployment problem in the United States. Even the farm-workers who had been homeless and hopeless since the dust bowl disaster now found themselves factory jobs, and for the first time in years, no longer had to struggle to survive.

91

This strong American support for Churchill was perhaps one of the reasons why Hitler finally gave up all thought of invading Britain, and turned to other ventures. In March, 1941, the German general Rommel attacked the British forces in North Africa, and forced them into full retreat. In April Germany invaded Greece and Yugoslavia, and on June 22, Hitler launched a full-scale attack on Russia.

Although neither Roosevelt nor Churchill had any fondness for the grim, brutal Russian leader, Stalin, Roosevelt blithely offered to extend the Lease-Lend arrangements to include Russia, and Churchill went on the radio promising Stalin all possible British aid. It was almost as though Churchill and Roosevelt were speaking with one voice, operating as a single team – and that began to apply to Britain and the U.S. as a whole.

By the summer of 1941, American destroyers were escorting British ships half-way across the Atlantic. If an American destroyer saw a U-boat, it immediately radioed the news to the British navy. Not surprisingly, U-boats began torpedoing American ships – and Roosevelt issued an astonishing order for the President of a nation at peace. If they saw a German ship that looked as if it might attack, American commanders were ordered to fire first, and ask questions afterwards!

On top of that, Roosevelt seized every German ship that happened to be in an American port.

All this could really mean only one thing.

Whether U.S. citizens liked it or not – though by this time, according to an opinion poll, most of them were cheering him on – their President was joining in the war.

92

10
 At War

Roosevelt was certainly being reckless. But then, he had always reacted to big emergencies by taking big risks . . . and never had he faced a bigger emergency.

The whole world seemed in danger of falling under a tyranny that would rule it for a thousand years, if Hitler's dreams came true – and by mid-1941, it looked as though they were doing just that. Austria, Czechoslovakia, Norway, Denmark, Holland, Belgium, France, Greece, Yugoslavia, Russia – all these countries had either been conquered by, or seemed about to be conquered by, their German invaders. Britain was still being ravaged by German bombers at home, and a British army was retreating in front of Rommel in the Western Desert. Japan's forces were making vast inroads into China – and Japan had just signed a pact with Germany and Italy. This pact – drawn up purely for the purpose of scaring America – warned that hostile action against any of those countries would mean war with all three.

Some Americans definitely were scared. 'Does any sane person,' asked ex-President Herbert Hoover, 'believe that we can defeat two thirds of the military power of the whole world?'

Roosevelt was probably encouraged to hear Hoover say that. He had proved that particular enemy wrong so often in the past!

Roosevelt's own incurable optimism remained as buoyant as ever. He remembered how he had given confidence to the whole United States at the moment when the nation had most needed it. Suddenly he decided on a grand gesture which would give new hope and new heart to every nation on the side of freedom.

Not caring in the least how it would look for a neutral President to confer with the Prime Minister of a nation at war, he arranged a meeting between himself and Winston Churchill. This took place in August, 1941, on board a destroyer off Newfoundland – water once again playing a part in Roosevelt's life. At this meeting, he and Churchill drew up a document called the Atlantic Charter.

This Charter made it clear that the U.S. was as much against Nazism as Britain – but it went further than that. After Hitler had been defeated, it said – defiantly ignoring the fact that Hitler's armies were at that moment undefeated anywhere in the world – the United States and Britain would work together to create a new era, in which all armaments were abolished, and 'all the men in all the lands may live out their lives in freedom from fear and want.' (In his fireside chats around this time, Roosevelt added two more freedoms – of speech and of worship – to be aimed at for every man, woman and child.) It was almost as if Roosevelt was trying to offer a New Deal to the whole human race, and many people now look back on the Atlantic Charter with a shrug of irritation or an embarrassed grin. What on earth were Roosevelt and Churchill doing, at one of the grimmest moments in history, concocting such a naive Utopian dream?

The answer is – they were achieving a great deal. The nations under German occupation – most of whose governments were in exile in London – desperately needed a flag to rally round; something to fight *for*, as well as *against*. A world where nations came together, not just for self-protection or self-interest, but to help all men and women to lead a fuller life – this was exactly the sort of hope that was needed.

From the day the Atlantic Charter was signed, people all over the world found their thoughts turning towards the new age that would dawn after the war. In Britain, under Churchill's government, schemes began to be drawn up for a new education act, and a complete Welfare State. In the U.S.A., the

Roosevelt and Churchill, immediately after signing the Atlantic Charter. Behind them: Admirals King and Leahy. (Peter Newark's Western Americana)

first diplomatic steps were taken which led to the forming of the United Nations – an organisation which has many faults and failings, but which over the years has quietly brought a great deal of relief to countless suffering people.

And all this began because of Roosevelt's extraordinary mind and personality.

Who else, in a world obsessed with terror, bloodshed and hate, would have dreamed of – let alone succeeded in – turning so many people's minds towards unity and peace?

*   *   *

The Atlantic Charter conference was the first of about a dozen meetings between Roosevelt and Churchill – meetings that eventually directed the whole course of World War II.

The two great men began by being half-scared of each other. The first thing Churchill asked his aides on returning to his boat was: 'Well? What did the President think of me?' And at that very moment, Roosevelt was asking his associates what Churchill had thought of *him*.

There was also a schoolboyish rivalry between them. Roosevelt boasted: 'I had thirteen warships at that meeting, but Winston only had two or three.' He added, with outright glee: 'Then one of his broke down, and *I* had to lend *him* a destroyer!'

Pretty soon disagreements developed. Roosevelt never ceased to be amazed by Churchill's grasp of the whole war scene, and unquestionably learnt a lot from Churchill about how a war should be planned and conducted. But he disliked what he considered Churchill's 'Tory' ideas. Britain still had a vast empire in those days, and Roosevelt could not resist occasionally suggesting that India, or Burma, or some other place, might one day want to be independent. He was also fond of lecturing Churchill on how Britain ought to do more to help the people in its colonies develop and improve themselves. Such remarks never failed to produce a roar of Churchillian fury, and could lead to hours of bickering.

Despite all this, there can be no doubt that the two relished each other's friendship. Churchill once said that just to meet Roosevelt was like opening a bottle of champagne. And Roosevelt summed up his feelings in a simple but stunning telegram, sent the day after one of their stormiest meetings.

'It's fun,' Franklin D. Roosevelt told Winston Churchill, 'to be in the same decade with you.'

*   *   *

Ironically, having started so many nations thinking about peace, Roosevelt now found himself hurtling towards war.

Japan had by this time finally allied itself with Hitler, and following his example, had overrun a great deal of China and Indo-China. Yet it still depended heavily on U.S. supplies of oil.

Roosevelt decided that this was a ridiculous situation. Here was the U.S. openly opposing Hitler, giving Britain all possible help short of war, and even supporting Russia against the Nazi invaders. How could it possibly go on supplying Hitler's Far Eastern ally with oil?

Roosevelt warned the Japanese that he would cut

97

off all trade with them, unless they took their troops out of China. Japan of course refused – and Roosevelt duly cut off the supplies of oil, although he knew that this would almost certainly make Japan attack, more especially so, since they now had a ferocious War Minister called Tojo.

At the beginning of December, 1941, the secret service, which had broken Japan's secret military codes and could decipher their radio messages, reported that a big attack was coming at any moment, but no one knew quite where. Strange as it seems now, no one at Washington dreamed that the Japanese would have the nerve to launch a head-on attack on the U.S. Pacific fleet, which was lying idly in a very exposed position in its main base at Pearl Harbor.

Some people say that Roosevelt himself never received these secret service reports. But it is probable that he did, and reacted in a typical Roosevelt way, by making a last-ditch stand for peace. On December 6, he sent an urgent 900-word personal plea straight to the Japanese Emperor, begging him to stop his ministers from spreading the War. To say that this plea did not work is to put it very mildly indeed.

The next day, on a cold but sunny Sunday afternoon when most U.S. citizens were lounging by their fires thinking about mailing their first Christmas cards, there came over the radio the most shattering news in the nation's history. Without anything remotely resembling a declaration of war, Japanese bombers had come streaking out of the blue and 'blitzed' Pearl Harbor. The whole truth, not revealed until much later, was even more shattering. They

Pearl Harbor – on December 7th, 1941, Japan attacked without warning and virtually destroyed the US Pacific Fleet. (Peter Newark's Western Americana)

had virtually wiped out the U.S. Pacific fleet. Of its eight battleships, one was blown up, three were sunk, and four were put completely out of action. A total of 177 Army and Navy planes were destroyed before they could even get off the ground, and more than 2,300 people were killed. On the same day, the Japanese had attacked U.S. forces in five other places: the Philippines, Wake Island, Guam, Thailand and Malaya!

The whole United States was stunned, including its President.

A day later, Roosevelt signs the declaration of war. (Oliver Yates Collection)

When he heard the news, Roosevelt said one word – 'No!' – and then spent a full eighteen minutes simply sitting, staring at the wall.

After that, he reached for the phone, and the U.S. was at war.

*   *   *

Four days later, Hitler – for once keeping a promise – supported his ally, and Germany declared war on the U.S.

Considering the size and prosperity of the U.S., this seems an extraordinarily reckless thing for the German dictator to have done; but he almost certainly thought that Roosevelt would be too busy fighting Japan to be much of a menace to Germany. He even doubted the U.S. ability to manufacture armaments. 'The Americans,' the Luftwaffe chief Hermann Goering had assured him, 'cannot build aeroplanes. They are only good at making refrigerators and razor blades . . .'

Roosevelt proved Hitler wrong on both counts.

Within a year of Pearl Harbor, the U.S. was turning out more guns, tanks and planes than the whole output of Germany and the conquered countries added together. At the famous Ford Willow Run plant near Detroit, in what was called 'the most enormous room in the history of man', a complete bomber was being manufactured in a single hour – and 8,760 in a single year!

Even earlier than that – within, in fact, a few days of Pearl Harbor – Churchill arrived in Washington for another conference, at which he argued that Japan should not, even now, be considered the main enemy. The greatest part of the American effort must continue to be used to help Britain against the Germans.

Only now, instead of giving all aid short of war, it would be all aid *including* war – with Americans marching side by side with the British both in Europe, and in Africa.

Considering that the U.S. had a deadly, multi-sided Japanese attack to cope with right on her doorstep, these proposals were very daring. Only Churchill would have had the nerve to make them.

You would have thought they would have led to hours of argument, if not bickering.

Yet Roosevelt – ignoring the shaking heads of many of his top military advisers – calmly, and almost instantly, decided that Churchill was right.

In the light of all that happened later, it can be said that that was the decision that really won the war.

11

 Victory
in Sight

Not that there was much war-winning during the next nine months. The U.S.A. had been caught off its guard, and took time to build up its strength. Meanwhile, the Japanese advanced relentlessly, taking Thailand, Wake, Guam, Hong Kong, Singapore and great stretches of Burma and Malaya. They also almost closed the Pacific to the U.S. fleet. At the same time, the British army in Africa continued to retreat before the Germans under Rommel, and in Russia, Hitler's invaders advanced almost within sight of Moscow.

But then, in October, 1942, the tide of war began, at long, long last, to turn against Hitler; and it was the British who turned it, winning the first outright victory of the war by routing Rommel's forces at the Battle of Alamein. Hard on the heels of this victory came the massive Russian triumph at Stalingrad, where a complete German army was captured; and at the beginning of 1943, the American general, Macarthur, recaptured New Guinea and Guadalcanal from the Japanese. Macarthur kept saying that he could do far more than this, if only Roosevelt would send him more men and ships.

But as we have seen, Roosevelt had agreed to Churchill's plan to make Hitler the main target, and once Roosevelt reached a decision, he never wavered.

American troops poured into Britain. (Eleanor Roosevelt, as usual acting as her husband's eyes and ears, popped across to visit them, and reported back to Roosevelt exactly what 'the boys' thought and felt.) American forces were also sent to North Africa, where the Churchill-planned operation, 'Torch', drove the Germans off the continent and opened the way for an Anglo-American invasion of Sicily and Italy.

In January, 1943, Churchill and Roosevelt met again – this time at Casablanca. Now there was no doubt that the war was being won. Roosevelt and his advisers were keen on launching an immediate cross-Channel invasion of Hitler's Europe, to finish it off as soon as possible – and the Russian leader Stalin was constantly sending messages to both Roosevelt and Churchill, begging them to start a 'Second Front'.

Churchill, though, was nervous. He wanted the big invasion of Europe to be postponed until more American troops could be amassed in Britain, and until Germany had been weakened by attacks elsewhere.

This anxiety of Churchill's was not, perhaps, surprising. After all, Hitler had been scared of launching a cross-Channel invasion at a time when he had countless divisions at his command, and Britain was defended largely by a Home Guard equipped with spades, pitchforks and broomsticks! Then, unlike Roosevelt, Churchill had been in the trenches in World War I. He knew from first-hand experience the terrible and endless slaughter that could result, if a German army was strong enough to dig itself in. He had also once been in partial charge

The War Directors – Roosevelt and Churchill at Casablanca, 1943, surrounded by their Chiefs of Staff. (Oliver Yates Collection)

of a sea invasion – at the Dardanelles, in 1915 – where things had gone disastrously wrong, and thousands of troops had been gunned down before their boats even reached the beaches. For all these reasons, and perhaps others, Churchill and his advisers pleaded with Roosevelt to wait until they were sure the invasion would succeed.

Roosevelt argued the point bitterly, but finally, he gave in, and agreed to postpone the invasion until 1944. (He realised, he said, that 'you don't walk down the street and buy a second front in a department store'.) He also accepted Churchill's suggestion that instead, an Anglo-American army should follow up the success of 'Torch' by invading Sicily and Italy.

This Churchill plan – attacking, as he put it, 'the soft underbelly' of Hitler's Europe – was put into action in the summer of 1943, and proved highly successful at first. Sicily collapsed in a fortnight, and so did the whole Italian government. But Hitler marched an army in to take over Italy, and suddenly the 'soft underbelly' was covered by an iron girdle. The Anglo-American army found itself with a long, bloody struggle on its hands. The top generals in Washington made it pretty clear that they thought Winston Churchill had blundered – and they began asking how much longer the U.S. was meekly to go along with every British suggestion! They even claimed that Roosevelt was being 'duped' by Churchill into using American troops to safeguard Britain – and worse, to prop up the British Empire in Africa.

Roosevelt paid no attention to these jibes. At least, he *appeared* to pay no attention. But he was never quite the same towards Churchill again.

At this point, a towering new figure appeared on the conference scene. Josef Stalin, the brilliant but devious leader of Communist Russia, announced that he would like to attend the next top-level meeting himself.

The first Big Three conference – between Roosevelt, Churchill and Stalin – occurred in November, 1943, at Teheran. With the leaders of Russia, America and the still-mighty British Empire all seated round the same table, never before in history had so much political power been assembled in one place.

The conference began with grand ceremonies. Churchill stood up and solemnly presented Stalin with a handsome sword, the gift of the King of

After D-Day – an American anti-tank gun in action against a German position in Europe. (Peter Newark's Western Americana)

England, as a tribute to the heroes of Stalingrad. Stalin proposed a toast to Roosevelt, as thanks for the Lease-Lend help to Russia. And both Stalin and Roosevelt wished Churchill a hearty 'Many Happy Returns' on November 30, his sixty-ninth birthday.

Roosevelt and Stalin appeared to get on very well together. Roosevelt was at his sunniest, and the Russian leader responded with a lot of chortles and hearty back-slapping.

Churchill found it difficult to join in. Although he had often praised Stalin as 'our gallant ally' and 'the great warrior', he was secretly suspicious of him.

Soon the conference ran into trouble. Churchill was still nervous about the proposed cross-Channel invasion of Europe, and kept suggesting that Germany should be attacked from the Italian side instead. Stalin poured scorn on Churchill's suggestions, and demanded that the cross-Channel project should go ahead as soon as possible. And Roosevelt, who was by now getting irritated by Churchill's caution, sided completely with Stalin. On one occasion, he and Stalin actually made fun of Churchill to his face, and the British Prime Minister only just stopped himself from stamping out of the room.

These quarrels were patched up, and Churchill, seeing himself outvoted, joined the others in drawing up plans for 'Operation Overlord', as the big invasion was to be called. It was suddenly clear that Churchill had been right in postponing it for so long. The whole project had a one hundred per cent greater chance of success in 1944 than it would have had in 1943. The German U-boats had been virtually beaten, and the U.S. could bring any amount of

The Third Man – Josef Stalin, the Russian leader, wanted to join the Churchill-Roosevelt conferences. Here he is with Roosevelt's special envoy, Harry Hopkins. (BBC Hulton)

supplies over to Britain across the Atlantic. The Luftwaffe had been driven clean out of the European skies. Stalin, whose armies were pressing the Germans very hard, was able to order a big offensive any time he wanted – and he deliberately ordered one the very week of Operation Overlord, to help his allies as much as he could.

The invasion was duly launched, on June 6, 1944 – a day which will always be remembered by its code-name, D-Day. Under the command of Dwight D. Eisenhower (a general picked by Roosevelt partly because he had a gift for getting on with the British) 150,000 men crossed the Channel in 4,000 ships, supported by 11,000 aircraft.

The Nazi empire did not give in easily. Months of bitter fighting lay ahead, including such tragedies as the Battle of Arnhem, where nothing was gained for a heavy loss of life. But the Allied armies established themselves in Europe, and from then onwards steadily and relentlessly began to drive the Germans back, freeing one occupied country after another. Stalin's armies began to advance equally irresistibly from the East. And the Americans were also scoring victories against the Japanese on the other side of the world.

At their next meeting – at Quebec, in September, 1944 – Churchill was already able to say to Roosevelt: 'Victory is everywhere'.

It may not have been everywhere, but it was certainly in sight.

* * *

Even at the darkest moment of the war, Roosevelt's mind had obstinately turned to thoughts and dreams of peace. Now, there was absolutely no holding him.

Leaving the conduct of the fighting mostly in the hands of his generals, he spent nearly all his time and energy planning a world in which war would be impossible, and there would be a 'New Deal' for all.

Just two months after D-Day, he arranged an international conference at Dumbarton Oaks, an old Colonial mansion near Washington. There, American, British, Russian (and, as a matter of fact, Chinese) delegates drew up detailed plans for a peace-keeping organisation to come into being as soon as victory was won. This was the real birth of the United Nations which, a year later, no less than fifty-one countries were to join.

Roosevelt believed, though, that the United

King and Supreme Commander. The American general Dwight D. Eisenhower talks to King George VI in France, 1944, after the successful Allied landings. (Peter Newark's Western Americana)

Nations would only succeed on one condition: that the U.S., Britain and Russia worked together as closely in peace as they had done in war. He even thought that their combined armies could act as a police force for the world! This did not seem to him an impossible idea. At the Teheran conference, he had found Stalin a jovial companion, surprisingly easy to bargain with, once one met him face to face.

He was confident that he could, as he put it, 'handle that old buzzard' – and he had, of course, no doubt that he could cope with Churchill too. As long as he, Roosevelt, was there, he was sure that the Big Three could become partners, and on this foundation, the United Nations could build a completely new age for all mankind.

As long as he was there . . .

That was the only real snag. Roosevelt had now been President of the United States for twelve years, holding down the world's most exacting job for longer than any other man in history. But now another Presidential election was due. Did he dare to run for a fourth term? Would his health stand the strain if he did?

He could not deny that there had been times lately when he felt he was cracking up – moments of dizziness when he had almost fainted. He knew, too, that his face had become pale and thin; that his hair had suddenly whitened, and that some of his closest friends were desperately worried about him. But he had a medical check-up, and the doctors could not find anything seriously wrong – nothing, at any rate, that they could put a finger on. On their evidence, he seemed to have stood up to twelve years of carrying the world on his shoulders extraordinarily well.

There was one other major factor that Roosevelt had to consider. The Republicans had chosen as their candidate a man, Thomas Dewey, who over the years had fought against everything Roosevelt stood for. He had even voted against Lease-Lend. What was worse, a great many Dewey supporters were Isolationist. In other words, they wanted the U.S. to 'mind its own business' and turn its back on the rest of the world, as it had done at the end of World War I. Roosevelt feared (with good reason) that if Dewey won, all his dreams of the Big Three working together, even of the United States joining the

The ailing victor. Roosevelt, tired but triumphant, after winning against Dewey. Beside him is Harry S. Truman, who succeeded him as President. Inset: *Thomas E. Dewey, who fought Roosevelt in the 1944 election, had attacked all that FDR stood for.* (Peter Newark's Western Americana)

United Nations, would be killed stone dead.

That settled it. Whether he was well enough or not, he *had* to stand.

With Roosevelt having brought the nation so close to victory in the war, you would have thought that the election would have been a walkover for him. But in fact, it turned out to be a very close-run fight – and a vicious one. Many businessmen hated Roosevelt so much that they were prepared to sack any employee who wore a 'Vote for FDR' button! A lot of employees replied by wearing Roosevelt buttons under their lapels, and Dewey ones on top. They would switch them over in the corridor or outside in the street, when they were leaving work at night.

The Republicans put it about that Roosevelt was in no condition to stand as President again: he was, they said, secretly desperately ill. (In this, they were nearer the truth than Roosevelt's own doctors.) Determined to scotch these rumours, Roosevelt recklessly drove down the centre of New York in an open car in freezing November rain. He was so angry with Dewey that he refused to relax for a second, and fought a fast and furious campaign all over the United States. You could almost say that he was finally doing a Theodore Roosevelt – he had a message to deliver, and would deliver it as long as there was breath in his body.

On the eve of the election, the Gallup polls were still giving Dewey the victory. But when it came to the point, the ordinary American people found that they just couldn't turn against this man whom they had come to look on as a close personal friend. Roosevelt got a smaller majority than in his previous three elections, but it was still a comfortable one.

He felt an overwhelming sense of relief. Now there was nothing to stop him bargaining with Stalin and Churchill, and guiding the world into peace.

He little dreamed that it was to be a peace that he would never see.

12

 The Day That Shook The World

In January, 1945, immediately after he was inaugurated for the fourth time as President of the United States, Roosevelt attended another Big Three meeting. This was held at Yalta, in the Crimea, since Stalin objected to leaving Russia.

There has probably never been a more important meeting in the whole of this century. First, it was to discuss how Russia was to join the United States in finishing off Japan. The atom bomb, which was to make this help unnecessary, had still not been fully developed at this time – and in any case, Roosevelt never had any intention of using it, except as a defence against an atomic attack by the Nazis. The decision to drop it on Hiroshima and Nagasaki, which ended the war against Japan so quickly, was made months later – by Harry S. Truman, Roosevelt's successor as President of the U.S.A.

Two other things were to be discussed at Yalta – and they weren't small things. They were the shape of the New Europe, and the creation of a peace to end all wars through the setting-up of the United Nations.

Three men – Roosevelt, Churchill and Stalin – were calmly trying to settle between them, at a single conference, the future of the greater part of the human race.

Franklin D. Roosevelt

It seems crazy now. It didn't seem so then. These three could claim to have organised between them the winning of a world-wide war. Why shouldn't it be within their powers to organise a lasting world-wide peace?

Roosevelt certainly went to Yalta in a supremely confident mood. He had absolutely no doubt that somehow he could persuade Stalin (and Churchill too, for that matter) to see things his way – the way of hope for all mankind. And the conference started well. Stalin was even more jovial than he had been at Teheran, and Roosevelt had no trouble in persuading him to agree to free, democratic elections being held all over Europe.

The Big Three at Yalta. Roosevelt, Churchill and Stalin at what has been called the most important meeting in the history of the world. But it was a meeting with disastrous consequences. (Oliver Yates Collection)

This was a vital point, because as the Russians rolled back the German army, they would be marching into country after country. Churchill suspected that they intended to *take over* those countries, and keep them under Russian rule for ever. He could already see what he was to call later 'an Iron Curtain descending across Europe'. Roosevelt, on the other hand, accepted Stalin's promise that that wouldn't happen. All his life, Roosevelt had tended to trust anyone with whom he'd shaken hands and talked matters over, face to face. He therefore solemnly agreed not to interfere with what the Russians were doing, and Churchill grudgingly went along with this agreement.

With one thing, though, Churchill definitely did *not* agree. Stalin demanded that Russia should take a large slice of Poland – and this met with roars of Churchillian fury. Hadn't Britain come into the war to rescue Poland from the Germans? Was it now to end with half the country being handed over to the Russians?

Roosevelt didn't really listen to Churchill's objections. Details like that could all be ironed out at a later Big Three meeting. What really mattered was that Stalin was friendly; that he was joining the war against Japan; that he was enthusiastic about the United Nations, and that he was promising free elections everywhere . . .

Roosevelt came away from Yalta still imagining that the conference had been a triumph. Churchill did not share this view by any means. He was more suspicious of Stalin than ever, and believed that if he and Roosevelt had teamed up closely, they could have prevented the Poland deal, and much more.

Now he wanted quick action to stop the Russians marching into any more countries than could be helped. If the Americans speeded up their advance, for example, they could easily free Czechoslovakia before the Russians got there. And if the British army pressed forward fast, they could race the Russians to Berlin. Roosevelt, though, would not agree to any of this. To him, the Russians were still gallant allies. The three nations were about to go forward side by side, first winning the war against Japan, then becoming partners in creating a golden world of friendship and peace. None of this would get off the ground if they didn't start by *trusting* each other!

So Russia was allowed to take Czechoslovakia, and to march across Germany right into Berlin – events which the world has bitterly regretted ever since.

Roosevelt was soon to have regrets himself. In February, 1945, he was still saying, with the old broad Roosevelt grin: 'Don't worry. I understand Stalin, and he understands me.' But by March, Stalin was already beginning to go back on some of his Yalta promises, and Roosevelt was forced to admit the possibility that the 'old buzzard' had been deceiving him all along.

As if that wasn't enough, Churchill was now very angry with him – and one or two messages he sent came close to threatening the end of the whole Anglo-American alliance. Roosevelt soon coped with that. He turned on his all-conquering charm. Friendly notes were exchanged, and in a few days, he was referring to Churchill as 'dear old Winston' once more. But his worries about Stalin went much,

The family President. Roosevelt with Eleanor and their thirteen grandchildren on January 20th, 1945, the day he became President for the fourth time. (Peter Newark's Western Americana)

much deeper. If Russia's word couldn't be trusted – if Churchill was right, and Stalin was going to seize all the countries he marched into – then all his, Roosevelt's, grand plans for peace would come to nothing.

And the sad, simple truth was that those grand plans were the only things that had been keeping Roosevelt going.

He felt suddenly not only tired, but totally exhausted. His face was grey; there were deep shadows under his eyes; his hands shook so much that he sometimes had trouble even signing his name. But underneath it all, traces of the old Roosevelt optimism were still there. All he wanted, he told himself, was a break. He needed to go somewhere to think things out – and he chose his favourite retreat, Warm Springs.

Sure enough, after a while there, he began to seem more cheerful. One day – April 11 – he posed for a big portrait, being painted to celebrate the beginning of his fourth term as President. He was wearing his blue naval cape – the sea was always there in the background of Roosevelt's life. He chatted and joked with the artist, a Mrs Shoumatoff. He flashed her the famous Roosevelt smile, and was careful to have his cigarette, in its long holder, at the jauntiest possible angle between his teeth. He made one surprising remark. He'd decided to take a long holiday, he said – and then resign the Presidency! 'If I can get the job, I'll head the United Nations instead,' he added.

He wasn't smiling when he said it, and no one in the room knew whether or not he was joking.

No one will ever know.

A quarter of an hour later, while still posing for the portrait, Franklin D. Roosevelt suddenly slumped forward in his chair, unconscious.

He did not recover consciousness again, and two hours later, he was dead.

*   *   *

April 11 was a day that shook the world. When the news was announced, around four in the afternoon, the whole United States was stunned. There were millions of young Americans who simply couldn't remember a time when anyone else had been President, and to many of them, it was like losing a father.

On Broadway, theatres and cinemas shut for the night. All over the country, signs appeared in shop windows: 'Closed. FDR Died.' Some even read: 'Closed – Death in the Family.' Everywhere on the streets – even in the fashionable Fifth Avenue, New York – one could see people walking along with tears streaming down their faces. One woman – an ice-cream seller – was asked why she didn't turn her radio on. 'For what do I need a radio?' she asked. 'The news is on everybody's face . . .'

London was also shaken. At Lloyd's the Lutine Bell was sounded, something that normally only happens when there is a great sea disaster. Winston Churchill, himself close to tears, wrote a personal note to Eleanor Roosevelt: 'I feel so deeply for you all. As for me, I have lost a dear and cherished friendship, forged in the fire of war . . .'

One could almost say that half the world, that day, felt it had lost a dear and cherished friend.

*   *   *

Roosevelt had died on the very threshold of peace. Victory over Nazi Germany was only four weeks away; victory over Japan less than sixteen weeks away. But the peace which Roosevelt himself had been working for – in which all men and women would have freedom of speech, freedom of worship, freedom from want and freedom from fear – was so far away that it was never to arrive at all.

If he had lived, it might have been a different story. Perhaps he might after all have found a way of getting round that 'old buzzard', Stalin, and made him keep his promises. Or perhaps with him as its leader, the United Nations might have become a real force to be reckoned with. Roosevelt had achieved the impossible so often in his life that it is hard to say what he might not have gone on to do.

He had conquered polio, and become President of the United States from a wheelchair.

He had taken over a beaten U.S.A., panic-stricken and on the brink of revolution, and turned it into the most powerful and prosperous nation on earth.

He had supported Britain through its darkest years, and taken the decision which saved the world from the worst tyranny that had ever threatened it.

Almost single-handed, he had created the idea of the United Nations, thus giving mankind its greatest – if at times inadequate – instrument of peace.

And he had died still searching for a miracle: a way to show the whole word (East and West) that it had nothing to fear but fear.

The world remembers – this Roosevelt statue in Grosvenor Square, London, was unveiled by Eleanor Roosevelt in 1948. The King and Queen and Winston Churchill were amongst those watching. (BBC Hulton)

Acknowledgements
and Thanks

I would like to thank Mr Peter Newark and the staff of his Western Americana Picture Library for the great pains they went to in finding photographs for this book. My thanks, too, to the BBC Hulton Picture Library, who also did considerable research on my behalf – and the London Borough of Sutton Public Library, who, as usual, came up at great speed with the many volumes I required.

Throughout this account of Roosevelt's life, I have been greatly indebted to the remarkable study *Roosevelt in Retrospect*, by John Gunther, a journalist who knew both Franklin and Eleanor personally (Hamish Hamilton, 1950); and Allen Churchill's lively history of the whole Roosevelt clan, *The Roosevelts* (Muller, 1966).

Other books providing me with either foreground or background facts for this story include:

Autobiography of Eleanor Roosevelt (Hutchinson, 1962)

New Deal and War: the LIFE History of the U.S., 1933–45 (Time-Life Books, 1964)

Generations of Americans (St. James Press, 1977)

Since 1900 Oscar Theodore Barck, Jnr and Nelson Manfred Blake (Collier-Macmillan, 1960)

The United States 1929–1945: Years of Crisis and Change Richard S. Kirkendall (McGraw-Hill, 1974)

Alistair Cooke's America (BBC, 1973)

Franklin D. Roosevelt

Eleanor & Franklin Joseph P. Lash (André
   Deutsch, 1971)
FDR's Last Year Jim Bishop (William Morrow &
   Co., 1974)
A History of the U.S.A. André Maurois
   (Weidenfeld & Nicholson)
Hitler vs. Roosevelt Thomas A. Bailey and Paul P.
   Ryan (Collier-Macmillan, 1979)

There is one last point. Winston Churchill forgot his
first meeting with Roosevelt in 1918. In my companion book to this one, *Winston Churchill: Never
Surrender*, I confess I forgot to mention it too!

December, 1980.   W.V.B.

Index

Index